THE ROAD
— TO —
RESILIENCE

The Billy Keenan Story

Billy Keenan

The Road To Resilience: *The Billy Keenan Story*

Jones Media Publishing
10645 N. Tatum Blvd. Ste. 200-166
Phoenix, AZ 85028
www.JonesMediaPublishing.com

Disclaimer:

The author strives to be as accurate and complete as possible in the creation of this book, notwithstanding the fact that the author does not warrant or represent at any time that the contents within are accurate due to the rapidly changing nature of the Internet.

While all attempts have been made to verify information provided in this publication, the Author and the Publisher assume no responsibility and are not liable for errors, omissions, or contrary interpretation of the subject matter herein. The Author and Publisher hereby disclaim any liability, loss or damage incurred as a result of the application and utilization, whether directly or indirectly, of any information, suggestion, advice, or procedure in this book. All stories are for entertainment purposes only and some names have been changed. Any perceived slights of specific persons, peoples, or organizations are unintentional.

Printed in the United States of America

ISBN: 978-1-948382-58-8 paperback

TABLE OF CONTENTS

INTRODUCTION

I am surrounded by darkness. I hear beeping noises. I feel my chest rise and fall as the air inflates my lungs every few seconds. I slowly begin to open my eyes; the darkness is pierced by a single fluorescent light. My eyes are wide open now and I start to look around the room. I see the silhouette of a shadowy figure toward my left side. I try to call, nothing but silence. I try to scream, nothing but silence. The shadow is now moving towards me. Everything is blurry. It must be the middle of the night because I would normally be wearing my glasses or contact lenses. The shadowy figure is now talking to me. I know this voice. It's my sister-in-law, Patty. I hear and feel the fear in her voice even though she is trying to speak calmly. In the flurry of words I can only make out "accident", "surfing", "paralyzed". It's the last word that I'm beginning to say to myself over and over and over. Paralyzed. Paralyzed. In complete denial I try to move. I try to move my legs. Nothing. I try to move my arms. Nothing. I specifically try to move my fingers. It feels like the bones of my hand are moving around through some kind of gelatinous liquid. I am in the grip of complete panic, the likes of which I have never known.

I close my eyes and try desperately to go back to the darkness. *Please God, let me go back into the darkness!*

I want to go back to that place of darkness where I was completely unaware of myself and my situation. Compared to where I am, darkness is beautiful. I am in and out of consciousness. I remember the dreams or hallucinations that I was having. I was on the beach, shirtless, wearing only my blue board shorts from the 7th Street Surf shop in Ocean City. All right, God...if I can be there right now. Ocean City is as close to heaven as there is. I want to be back in Mom's condo on West Avenue and 45th St., waking up at 6 AM putting on those blue board shorts and flip-flops, looking into my sons' bedroom to see their beautiful little red heads peeking out from under the covers, in the kitchen, pouring myself a travel mug of coffee. My surfboard is already on the roof rack of my Honda Odyssey and I drive a few minutes to 59th St. and Central Avenue. This is the spot. After a few stretches, I finish my coffee and start to run toward the ocean, my feet barely touching the sand. I feel like a child running to see Santa Claus. The water is warm and refreshing as I paddle out through the waves. The sun is coming up and a pod of dolphins is just to my right. I am in heaven. Suddenly, my head and back were lying in the sand, but my legs were up on the bench of a picnic table. Next I was apologizing to my wife because I spent $12,000 on a Steinway grand piano that was once played by Roy Bittan from the E Street band.

In the final hallucination that I remember I was unable to move and thought that I was shackled on a ship bound to Australia. I was an Irish rebel being sent to Van Diemen's land. I can make out the voices of my captors and want only to free myself from the shackles and free my comrades. The voices I heard were not British soldiers but rather the nurses who were running in and out my room.

It is daytime and my wife has arrived at the hospital. The gaps in the story are now being filled. I can't remember if it was her or someone else from the medical staff who told me the extent of my injury. I had fractured cervical spine 1, 2, 3, 5, and 6. I also suffered a spinal cord contusion at the level of C4. Additionally, because of the severity of my injury, I had suffered a right vertebral artery occlusion. Again, I try to move; this time my attempts are met with excruciating pain emanating from my head. There is some kind of metal brace encircling my head. It seems to be attached with metal screws going into my skull. My prison is not just psychological, it is physical. One of the nurses is reading my lips and tells me it is called a "halo". I immediately flashed back to the time when my cousin Peter Dolan suffered a traumatic brain injury while he was in college. He had to wear a halo for many months and there are still indentations where the screws were. I now know why I have a halo. The purpose is to completely immobilize my head and neck.

It is Friday and I have been unconscious for two weeks. One of the nurses is telling me that they kept me in a coma for two weeks so that I would not try to move. "I lost two weeks of my life! I missed Larry Bennett's 90th birthday party. I missed Mary Cooney's 100th birthday. I missed Tommy Maloney's tailgate party at West Point!". This was a party for a thousand people thrown by Billy Colbert the CEO of Tommy Maloney's Meats. The money would have been great for this job, but even more than that it would have given my band incredible exposure and the opportunity for really high-paying jobs. "I have to get out of this and get back to work! I've got to get back to playing with the band!". I know my wife is in the room. She's talking to the medical staff while I am lying on my back with this crown of thorns, with tears coming down my cheeks.

I'm desperate. I have only just begun to count my losses.

Apparently, my wife has been in the hospital at my bedside for the last two weeks. She left only when our son Kieran burned his mouth with hot chocolate and was crying out for his mother. She is going on and on about what happened in those first terrible hours. She tells me that her friend Jane was outside in the van with our sons and ultimately that her father and brother came to take Patrick and Kieran home. She immediately called my brother Jim who was at West Point with my brother John for an Army football game. Everyone was at a post-game tailgate party when she told my brothers that I was in a terrible accident. She told them to bring my mother.

Before she could continue, a nurse came in with a liquid that she poured through a feeding tube into my stomach. "What the hell is this?", I thought to myself. Again, I was trying to ask the question of what was happening, but of course the silence continued. I made the only noise that I could make to get someone's attention. I pursed my lips and blew out, making a farting noise. My wife came to my bedside and I asked, "What is happening?". She struggled to read my lips. I tried again, "Tell me!". My eyes are wide open and I am looking around the room desperate for an answer. She realizes what I am asking. "You have a trach and ventilator for your breathing so you cannot swallow." *I cannot swallow? How can I not swallow?*

Is this how I am going to be for the rest of my life? *What kind of life is this?*

Does this mean I will never be able to eat solid food again? My wife is going back and forth between my bedside and the nurses' station. There is never a moment when she focuses on me. She never puts her hand through the metal halo to stroke tears away from my eyes and tell me, "I love you. It's a miracle that you are here and I will be by your side no matter what." —words that I was hoping to hear. This moment never happens. Meghan went into her clinical nurse mode and a matter-of-fact manner. This must have been her defense mechanism to try to keep me from losing my shit.

I asked my wife who read my lips, *"Where are the boys? Are they okay? Are they asking where I've been the last two weeks of their lives? Will I ever be able to put my arms around them again?"* I know I have to banish these thoughts from my mind and concentrate on what is going on right now in this room. How will I live from this minute to the next?

She answers, "They are okay. My parents moved to our house immediately after your accident." I feel relieved to know that they are okay. *What must they be thinking?*

A male nurse enters the room and tells me, "Bill, I am going to roll you over on your side and use a cupping technique to loosen the mucus in your lungs." Now I am over on my right side and he is pounding on me repeatedly almost like someone playing the bongos. After five minutes of this treatment, they use suction to pull out the secretions from my lungs. They tell me that because I was submerged in the ocean for so long, I now have pneumonia.

My wife is now telling me that they performed the surgery to fuse C5 – 6 together. She had waited hours to give the go ahead for the surgery that the doctors in the trauma center recommended because she was waiting to hear from a family friend who was a neurosurgeon. He made a recommendation for surgery after he viewed the MRI. I don't understand why she would not take the recommendation of the doctors at the trauma center over some Irish guy in Las Vegas. That notion got shoved quickly to the side as there was so much other stuff going on in my room. Now, they are sliding me onto the stretcher to go back for another MRI.

As we roll down the corridor, I see a window and notice that it is nighttime. Since I woke up on Thursday morning in the middle of the night, this must be Friday night but I'm not sure. There is a nurse and an aide walking me through the hospital to the elevator to get me to the MRI. They start asking me questions about how I got hurt. I mouthed, "I was in a surfing accident." The aide tries to read my lips but can't understand, so he keeps asking, "What happened to you? Were you in an accident?"

The nurse jumps in and says, "Stop!" I feel a sense of relief; this line of questioning is more than I can face. The MRI staff gently moves me from the stretcher to the MRI table. They try to manipulate my arms to go upwards through the machine over the Halo but it is absolutely impossible. I feel excruciating pain coming from the black steel bars in my back every time they try to manipulate my arms. The pain I am feeling is coming from the frame of the Halo that rests on my back. The pain emanates from my shoulders since I cannot feel below the site of my injury. These words, "below the site of my injury" are all new to me and still make no sense. I am a surfer, triathlete, musician, batting practice pitcher, and swim coach.

I am back in my hospital room and my brothers Jim and John have come down to relieve my wife so she can go home and care for our children. I start to ask my brothers the difficult question. "How do I urinate? How do I defecate?" Jim tells me that I urinate with the use of a catheter inserted in my penis. They tell me I defecate when they roll me over and insert a small enema into my rectum. They wait for close to 30 minutes and I defecate onto a pad. The rest of the time I am in an adult diaper. Once again, when I thought it could not get worse, it did. I am in a freaking diaper! "How is this even possible?" I asked no one but myself. *"Please God, let me go back to the darkness!".* What kind of life is this going to be? I cannot move my arms or legs. I cannot control my bodily functions. With all of this, the visitors who come during the ensuing days all seem overjoyed that I am alive. I cannot share in their joy.

Gift cards, money, and offers of all kinds of assistance arrive daily at the trauma center. I drift in and out of consciousness. My brothers leave for a while to get dinner. When they return they tell me they ate. I'm filled with rage that I am still being fed through the feeding tube and not able to enjoy all the great food that they had for dinner. Once I settle down, it's time to try to get some sleep. My brothers settle down to sleep quickly, but I'm kept awake by the bright fluorescent light just outside my room. I make my raspberry sound several times before my brothers wake up. In the dark, they try to read my lips as I try to scream, "The light! The light!" They have no idea what I am talking about and try to guess. "Yes, it is nighttime. Try to get some sleep." Now, in fury I make my raspberry sound again and mouth the words "Close the curtain! Close the curtain!" After what seems like an eternity, one of my brothers realizes that they have to hold the curtain in front of the fluorescent light so I can get to sleep. My sleep is fitful, tormented, and comes in short bursts through the night. I dream that I am in a casino with red velvet carpet and the beeping sounds of slot machines, but of course, it is my ventilator. I pray for the darkness. This is a tender mercy that never comes. The next morning, my brothers excitedly show me the CaringBridge website. Over 1000 people have sent messages of prayers and good wishes to me. I am overwhelmed by the sheer number of people responding to my injury. This news bolsters my spirits for at least a few moments. Meanwhile, my wife has been pushing the medical staff to move me from The New Jersey Shore Medical Center in Neptune to Helen Hayes Hospital in Stony Point, New York, a short 10-minute drive from our home. The medical staff insists on patience because they feel that I am too weak to travel..

It is now October 2nd, and something quite miraculous has occurred. Typically, when someone has my injury, they are completely dependent upon the ventilator for breathing. Seemingly out of nowhere, the respiratory therapist was in my room and she called out, "He's breathing above the vent! Billy is breathing above the vent!"

This news sets off a flurry of events with nurses and doctors coming in to see what was going on. Rather than having my entire body wait to be filled with oxygen, I was taking a partial breath! No one ever expected this to happen. At this point, the chances of my breathing independently were remote at best, but this event was the first and only sign of encouragement since my injury. Once again, my wife pushed for transfer to Helen Hayes Hospital. This time, the medical staff, most notably the director of the trauma center, agreed. The director Dr. Patrick was a great guy. Ever since my awakening he has been a constant presence in my room. His bedside manner is so different from some of the younger physicians. Dr. Pat is in his mid-fifties and takes the time to talk to me about my interest in music, physical fitness, and history. He takes the time and patiently tries to read my lips as we have our long drawn out conversations. He tells me that he and his kids have just finished the Tunnel to Towers Run in New York City. I smile and mouth the words "I wish I could've been there!" I will never forget, from now until my dying day, the exact words that Dr. Pat said to me when he found out that I was breathing above the vent. He looked at me and spoke to me like a coach sending in the last play of the Super Bowl when he said, "Billy, this is your Olympics! Your physical and occupational therapy are important, but your respiratory therapy is most important. You have a slight chance of regaining independent breathing. I don't know if it's possible but you must treat this like it is your Olympics. Promise me!"

I looked at Dr. Pat, my eyes beginning to tear up and mouthed the words, "I promise! I promise!". The promise I made to the doctor is one that I've been making to myself for my entire life. I made the promise to give everything I had to adapt, and to overcome adversity, trauma, and major life changes. This is resilience. This is the force that has propelled me to the best of times and through the very worst of times.

---------- CHAPTER 1 ----------

BORN TO BE...

Like most boys, I wanted to be just like my father. My Dad was a New York City Police Department (NYPD) detective, but he was also a great Irish accordion player, singer, and step dancer. Some of my earliest memories are of my dad playing and singing at family parties. By the age of two, I was standing upright, holding onto the rails of my crib singing Irish songs like "The Old Maid in the Garrett" by Sweeney's Men. At the age of two, I got my first guitar. The instrument was plastic, had no strings, and I would bring it with me to the Saturday evening folk Mass at St. Anthony's Church in The Bronx. The music for the liturgy consisted of acoustic guitars and tambourines, and I would stand on the bench strumming my stringless guitar, singing along to the howls of laughter of my fellow congregants.

The Bronx of my parents' youth started to change in the late nineteen sixties, so in 1970, my father made the decision to move the family to "the country." My dad's oldest brother, Matt, settled in Stony Point, New York and so we followed him. Stony Point in the 1970s was a place where kids had the run of the neighborhood. There was no such thing as playdates, and we would ring our friends' doorbells until we found enough guys to get a game up of whatever sport was in season. We shot BB guns, built forts, and crapped in the woods, and basically lived a good portion of our childhood out of adult supervision. We got into fistfights and were friends again with our opponent within minutes. My brothers and I were classic Catholic school kids. Immaculate Conception Parish and its grammar school were a huge part of our lives. It wasn't just a school. Here, the nuns and faculty looked out and cared for us above and beyond what most teachers do. Our Parish family consisted of people of mostly the same socioeconomic status. Stony Point was not a rich town. It was more a solidly middle class town, made up of children and grandchildren of immigrants who were living their American dream. It was a great place to grow up.

All I wanted as a boy was to play music with my father. At the age of 8, I begged for tin whistle lessons. The assigned tune for the first week was "Dawning of the Day." After struggling to learn the tune for an hour, I wanted to give up. Without a word, my father went to his room and got his accordion. He played the tune slowly for me, and stuck with me until I had it. Once I got the tune, a whole new world was opened up to me. With my father's help, and some resilience, I was able to reap the reward of a lifetime of music. Within a month, I was sitting in front of the family stereo and was learning tunes by ear. I quickly progressed to flute. When I transitioned to flute, I was required to learn musical notation. Reading music simply slowed me down; all I needed was to hear the tune and I could play it back very quickly. This is the way Irish musicians learn tunes. The problem with the flute is that you can't sing, and I loved to sing!

My brother Jimmy had already given up the fiddle for guitar, and he taught me to play the guitar. At a garage sale we bought a Beatles songbook for $1 and proceeded to learn every song in the book. We sat face to face with two guitars, learning the chords and forming the basis of harmonies that are completely unique to people who share the same DNA like the Everly Brothers or Brian, Karl, and Dennis Wilson of The Beach Boys.

At the age of 14, my brother Jim and I wanted to start our first band and I was asked to learn the bass guitar. I found a teacher named Jimmy Kineally who asked me, "Bill, what do you want to learn?" I told Jimmy, "I want to be a singing bass player just like Paul McCartney or Sting". So each week I brought a cassette recording of the song I wanted to learn; we picked out the bass part, and by the end of each hour, I had mastered the notes and vocals for each song. Jimmy Kineally was the perfect bass teacher. He was a working musician who made his living playing in a wedding band. Under his tutelage, I learned to play and sing a variety of songs that would serve me well in the future.

"The force is strong in you, young Jedi!" Jimmy told me that day. This kind of compliment was music to my ears. I already had a very strong Irish repertoire thanks to my dad's record collection and playing music and singing at every family party. I remember vividly playing with my Dad and my brother Jim at our grandfather's 90th birthday party. We played a few Irish songs and then I launched into "I Love a Rainy Night" by Eddie Rabbitt. I heard a roar go up from the crowd and people started moving to the dance floor. I felt a complete rush of adrenalin, the kind of feeling that you could chase for your entire lifetime.

I was born to be a musician. It did not matter whether there was an audience, or I was just by myself, I simply love to make a "joyful noise". Even at this early age, I was learning to use music to express the emotions that I was feeling at the time. My father always used to say, "There will be a time when you won't be able to play sports anymore. Music, however, you will be able to play for the rest of your life." These words from my father, the man who brought me into the music, would ring true for the rest of my life.

The Irish Way

It was during that magical Summer of 1983 when this 16-year-old became "Irish". My parents gave me the greatest gift, and they sent me on–a six-week cultural study program called "The Irish Way." I joined 120 high school juniors and seniors at Gormanston College in County Meath. Our days were filled with classes in Irish History, Irish literature and poetry, Irish language, and

Irish music and dance. I packed my guitar, tin whistle, and soccer gear. After the first full day of classes, we had a talent show. It was meant to be an icebreaker, but nobody wanted to break the ice. I pulled my guitar out of the case and, with great confidence, took a seat in front of 120 of my peers. I closed my eyes and softly started to sing a song about the troubles in Northern Ireland. I felt a hush come over the room as I sang "Only Our Rivers Run Free". I opened my eyes at the end of the song and the hush was broken by rapturous applause. I stood up to make my way back to my seat, but everyone screamed for more. I felt the rush of connecting with an audience of my peers, so now I knew that the next six weeks were going to change my life.

The Irish Way afforded me a certain degree of independence and freedom. Early on in the course, I met a beautiful girl from Bethel, Connecticut. One slow dance on Friday night was all it took to find my first real girlfriend. Far from the prying eyes of parents, we took long walks on the beach by the Irish Sea, walked around Dublin, hand in hand and did a lot of kissing. It was an innocent "first love." Being away from home, yet feeling completely at home, is best expressed in a line spoken by Tom Cruise's character in the movie "Far and Away" – "I am of Ireland."

The trip opened my eyes to a wider world. I found that I had the ability to make friends from all over the United States and be completely comfortable in their company. Due to my ability to play soccer, I was welcomed by the locals and included in all of their matches. Most importantly, I realized at the tender age of 16 that I could fearlessly try new things and that realization would have a significant effect on the rest of my life.

The God Card

During the spring semester of Junior year, there was an announcement about auditions for the school play, *Fiddler on the Roof*. I had enjoyed musical theater during my elementary school years, but in high school drama and sports did not mix.

Unfortunately my Mom got wind of the audition and laid the ultimate guilt trip on me.

"Billy," she said, "God gave you the ability to sing and to act. If you don't try out for the play it will be an insult to God."

"Well shit," I thought to myself, "she played the God card." I agreed to audition. I was cast in the lead role of Tevye in *Fiddler on the Roof*. I hate to say it, but Mom was right. I absolutely loved musical theater but had suppressed it for fear of being considered a nerd.

Just before the play opened, we did a dress rehearsal for the whole student body. I stood on that stage and sang and danced my way through "If I Were a Rich Man." The applause was thunderous and the whole school saw a different side of me. My debut was not only accepted but celebrated. My heart felt like it was going to explode with joy. The play was a smashing success and the celebrity that came along with the starring role had unintended wonderful effects.

I was blessed with a talent, a gift from God. In order to show Him gratitude for this gift I had to find the courage to get up and perform for my peers. For the first two years of high school I kept that hidden.

The experience left me with the feeling that I had more to give so I threw my hat in the ring for student council president. I had a few weeks to campaign for the election and brought together a group of my most trusted advisors (my soccer teammates) for a campaign meeting. During that meeting we generated over 50 hilarious campaign posters, and I won in a landslide.

With each success, my life was changing fast. Prior to my senior year, I brought together the student council officers and we mapped out a plan for the year that would incorporate service and loads of fun for the entire student body. At the same time, I started to think about my future and that maybe all of these things were leading me to pursue a life of service to something bigger than myself. One of the things that I was starting to consider was a career as an Army officer. For some reason, I had been given these abilities and made the most of every opportunity. I felt the sense of obligation to serve and to lead.

At the end of Junior year I was selected to attend the American Legion Boys State at Siena College, a week-long leadership convention where the best and brightest high school seniors from across NY State form their own government. Every morning we were awakened by members of the US Marine Corp Reserve for physical training. I had never marched in cadence or responded to an order to exercise in cadence by a Marine in uniform. An experience that most of my friends would have rejected, I embraced wholeheartedly. While the early wake up calls were new to me, the morning workouts were easy compared to my life as a soccer player. The experience at Boys State would lead me to one of life's next major decisions.

The Calling

Throughout high school, my favorite subject was history. Some of the topics covered were the World Wars, the Korean conflict and the Vietnam War. When we got to the Cold War, I began to see the evils of the single party Marxist dictatorship and the contrast between democracy and capitalism. I was 16 years old and listened intently to the speeches of Ronald Reagan. I was deeply influenced by one young man who had gone to West Point and another who had joined to ROTC (Reserve Officers Training Corps).

At midnight Mass during my Senior year of high school, I saw a boy from our parish named Jim Kitz in his dress gray uniform from West Point. During the whole Mass I could not take my eyes off of him, the way he stood and moved and how everyone in the Church viewed him. After Mass, I got to speak to him briefly and asked him how he liked his life at West Point, and he said "Billy, it's the hardest thing I've ever done and I love it." After Mass we returned home to open our gifts and my Dad was still talking about how impressed he was with Jim Kitz. I wanted my father to look at me the same way.

The second was my cousin, Michael Dolan. Michael and I always had a very special relationship. Of all of my cousins, I looked up to him the most and tried my very best to be just like him. Michael was a football player, an honor student, and a deeply devout Catholic. As a senior at Washingtonville High School, he applied for a Marine ROTC scholarship to the Citadel in Charleston, SC. When Michael graduated from the Citadel he was awarded the Wilson Ring, voted by his classmates to be the manliest, most courageous, and most admired in his class.

They were good students, good athletes, and young men of high character. I believed that I had these qualities and wanted to see if I had what it took to serve in the very same way. My decision to attend Fordham University on an ROTC scholarship was an example of where my head and my heart were guiding me.

I was accepted to Fordham University, but rejected for an ROTC scholarship. Therefore, I entered Fordham as a regular student. I loved every aspect of my life at Fordham, but I had forgotten "the calling." Consequently, in the words of Dean Wormer from Animal House, I got "fat, drunk and stupid" and had the grades to show for it. Over the mid-semester break, my father sat me down and said "You've got one semester to show that you deserve this. If you don't improve your grades, you'll be at community college. Your Mother and I have not been on vacation in four years, and our cars need to be replaced, but we're sacrificing all of this to send you to Fordham". I never forgot or wanted to see the look of disappointment in my father's eyes again.

The fear of life as a commuter at a community college was enough to jar me into action. When I returned to Fordham for the second semester, I enrolled in the American Red Cross Lifeguard class and spent two nights a week in the pool. At night I would put on a pair of sweats, a rubber shirt to melt away the beer weight, and a hoodie and run around the campus. My jumprope became my best friend, inspired by the main character in the movie *Vision Quest*. A wrestler who needed to lose weight achieved his goal, using his jump rope to get there.

At the end of the first year, I took the NYS lifeguarding exam and got hired as a lifeguard at Lake Welch. Every week we were required to do running and swimming. When I returned to Fordham to begin sophomore year, I was a completely different guy.

Everything turned around when I became friends with Jay King and Joe Clark, two ROTC cadets who lived on my floor. One morning during the first semester, I got up, got dressed, and walked to the ROTC building. I entered the office and an officer came out to see if I needed help. I looked at him and said "Sir, my name is Bill Keenan and I want to be a Lieutenant in the United States Army." The officer reached out his hand and said, "Welcome Bill, my name is Captain Tom Woodley. Come into my office and sit down."

Captain Woodley encouraged me to apply for a two-year scholarship. A few short weeks later, I was talking with Captain Woodley when Major Fred McGarry (a retired police officer who knew my Dad well) informed me that my scholarship board interview would be that day. I begged off saying "Sir, this is not the best time. My initial reaction was, "could I come back in a few hours?" He said, "Bill, don't worry it's only going to take 10-15 minutes." What he didn't know was that under the collar of my denim jacket was a massive hickey given to me by an overzealous companion. When I walked into the board interview, they asked me to get comfortable and take off my jacket. I had to answer the questions of the board while looking at them smiling and doing their best to not laugh. To my amazement, I got the scholarship.

I would have to attend cadet basic camp at Fort Knox Kentucky the summer after sophomore year. Everyone at basic camp was a college student entering ROTC and ultimately would become a Second Lieutenant. We lived in barracks, and drill sergeants were our primary instructors. Each week I received letters from my fellow lifeguards at Lake Welch Beach telling me they were taking care of all the female lifeguards. This was the first of many sacrifices I would have to make, but it was there I discovered a love for military life and my calling.

It was another powerful force leading me to pursue a life of deliberate discomfort* as an Army officer. All great civilizations have hero archetypes that they look to for inspiration. In my family I didn't have to look any further than my grandfather John Keenan. At the age of 12, he lost his mother and at 16 left Ireland bound for New York where two of his brothers had settled. He spent his first year in America working as a farm hand in Port Jervis, NY. In 1917 with the entrance of the United States into the first World War, my grandfather put down his pitchfork and enlisted in the United States Army, even though he was not yet a citizen. He ended up in France seeing active combat in World War One. He remained a bachelor until the age of 42 and married a woman aged 24 from the same part of Ireland from which he came. Together they had ten children. Five of the six boys served in either the Army, Navy or Marine Corp. Military service was never forced on me, but I was taught from the earliest age that there was no higher calling. *The phrase "deliberate discomfort" was inspired by the book "Deliberate Discomfort" by Jason Van Camp, a Special Forces soldier.

CHAPTER 2

MONEY FOR NOTHING!

My Father's brother Matty was a cop in the 50th precinct near Manhattan College, and there was a young police officer named Michael Sheahan who worked there. Mike had his own band and Matty told him about me every chance he got. Finally, Mike gave in and I got the call to come down to his house for an audition. Mike was American born, but occasionally spoke with a brogue, especially when speaking with any Irish born person. He was a brilliant musician who played seven instruments to accompany his fantastic voice. I stepped off the bus near Mike's home on Katonah Avenue, in the Woodlawn section of the Bronx, with my guitar and bass in hand. I began my audition by playing and singing "The Fields of Athenry". Mike immediately picked up his mandolin to accompany me and sang in harmony with me. A partnership was forged by the end of that song. For the next two hours, I ran through my Irish repertoire and then switched to bass for some rock and roll music. I got the gig and the band picked me up at Fordham a few days later. From that moment on, I was making $300 a week through my next three years of college. My first performance with Mike's band "The Variety Show Band" was at a bar in Clifton, NJ. We played a good mix of Irish and American tunes, and the dance floor was full for the whole night. I had my bass guitar around my neck, and when I sang the lead vocal in "Twist and Shout", I experienced a high I had never before experienced before. During the break, I found out that the band could eat and drink for free. The drummer, a fellow from County Kerry, ordered a turkey club and I ordered the same. I had a few pints of Harp and arrived back at Fordham with $125 in my pocket.

I tapped into the experience of the members of the band who were all considerably older than me. My musicianship and competence as a performer grew rapidly. The band leader Mike and I rehearsed frequently in order to add songs to our repertoire. We worked very hard to make it look easy. Every time I finished a gig and got paid, it felt almost like a surprise. I loved performing so much that half the time at the end of a gig I was on such a high I'd forget I was getting paid. I was splitting my time between Fordham, ROTC, and the world of Irish Music. I was spending so much time around Irish people that it reignited the fire I felt during Irish Way. I soon felt myself becoming very "Irish".

The music touched my heart and soul. The words of the songs and the stories they conveyed touched me deeply–songs about immigration, the pain of loss, and the feeling of patriotism. I never considered what my peers thought about my playing Irish music. I stuck with the music even during my teenage years when many Irish musicians gave it up because it wasn't "cool". By the time I got to college, my roommates thought it was the coolest thing in the world. Getting paid to play Irish music in the pubs and drinking free beer WAS the coolest damn thing in the world. The best perk of being the guy with the guitar was that girls were everywhere.

The thrill I got from being part of that first band never really went away in all the years I played. There's nothing to compare to the rush you feel when performing with your mates, everything clicks, and the dance floor is packed on a Saturday night at an Irish wedding. The band was so together and well-rehearsed that the music just flowed. We made it look so easy. My musical ability stayed with me through every chapter of my life and connected me with amazing people. At this point the music was now entirely a part of me.

During my four years at Fordham, lifeguarding and ROTC workouts kept me in great physical shape. My life as a professional musician enabled me to buy my first car. I was never without pleasant female company and enjoyed several long-term relationships during college. The academic rigor from both Jesuit and layman professors had prepared me to do life's most essential task, which is to think. I was ready for life's next challenge.

No Retreat, No Surrender

I graduated from Fordham in May of 1989 with a degree in Communications and a Commission as a Second Lieutenant in the US Army. The pictures from that day show me with my family, smiling. Inside, however, I was in absolute agony. At the beginning of senior year, I had requested an active duty commission. However, in early January, Captain Woodley, gave me the bad news.

"Bill, I'm sorry. Your commission is going to be in the Reserves." I hung up the phone, went to my bedroom and broke down. My Dad came in, sat down with me, put his arm around me, and tried to comfort me, but I was beyond consolation. I felt like my beating heart had been ripped out of my chest. The only thing I wanted to do was to serve on active duty and now it felt like I was being judged and found unworthy. The reality was that my last medical exam showed a hernia and the Selection Board thought it best for me to spend the rest of my time in the Reserves. During my second semester of senior year, I went through the motions enjoying my music life and time with my friends, but in truth I was running on fumes. After graduation, I returned home and lifeguarded for the summer at Lake Welch.

Every new U.S. Army Second Lieutenant, whether active or reserve, has to attend a five month long active duty course called The Officers Basic Course, or OBC. On August 15th, I said goodbye to all my friends at Lake Welch and drove to Hopewell, VA. Our class was made up of roughly 80 lieutenants, both active and reserve. I started making friends very quickly and fell in with a small crew of guys that I would spend many good times with in the ensuing months. One day early on in the course, our class commander Captain Jerry Reeves, a good ole boy from the South, announced, "The top two reserve officers in our class will be automatically offered active duty commissions. The criteria will be exams, leadership, a physical fitness test, and an interview with a Review Board." I could hardly believe what I was hearing. My heart practically jumped out of my chest. I again had hope that I could achieve my dream. I started looking around the classroom to see if there were other lieutenants thinking the same thing that I was. These guys would be my competition. Could I beat them? Could I be the one?

Like a gambler with nothing to lose, I pushed all my chips into the center of the table and went after an active duty slot. Even if I did everything right, there was no guarantee of success. Would I be able to deal with another rejection? I decided that I had already survived rejection once, what was one more time? I did everything in my power, spending extra hours working out and running. I even skipped a night or two of drinking in the Officers' Club with my buddies to study for exams. The final step in the process was the Review Board.

I woke up pre-dawn and went to work on my uniform and shoes. My ribbons and insignia were in perfect position. You could see your reflection perfectly in my shoes. When it came my turn, I marched confidently to a position exactly four feet from the table behind which sat three officers, two Majors and one Lieutenant Colonel. I brought my right hand up to my eyebrow and saluted the Chairman of the Review Board and said, "Sir, Lieutenant Keenan reports". He returned my salute and motioned for me to sit down. The two Majors asked several questions, all of which I felt that I had answered perfectly. The Chairman of the Board, the Lieutenant Colonel, asked the final question, "Why do you want to serve on Active Duty?"

"Sir, one weekend a month and two weeks in the Summer will never be enough for me. I want to do this every single day. I have so much more to give." My answer blew them away. I even saw the Lieutenant Colonel sit up a little straighter when he heard the second part of my answer. Twenty minutes later, Captain Reevese came over to me and told me I did it. I passed the test. My active duty service changed the trajectory of my life. I was going to be a leader of troops in the greatest army in the world. I had no idea where I was being called to serve. I only knew that whenever I was needed, wherever I was needed, and whatever was required of me, I would do.

Just as I had been rejected for a ROTC scholarship out of high school, I had been rejected for an active duty commission out of college. However, I did what I had always done in the face of adversity or failure. Several times in my young life I answered a critical question. "What are you willing to do to achieve your goal? Are you willing to give it one more try with no guarantee of success? Are you willing to risk getting rejected one more time? Each time, I fearlessly pushed all my chips into the center of the table. I went "all in". I dug deep to turn defeat into victory. I was on the road to resilience!

Jump School

In mid-January 1990, I attended the US Army Airborne school at Fort Benning Georgia. Earning Airborne wings is a right of passage for most 2nd Lieutenants. Airborne school is a three week course that culminates in five jumps from Air Force aircraft from a height of 1500 feet. The first two weeks of the course, ground and tower week, are the difficult parts– 4:30 AM wake-ups and 5 AM PT sessions for 1 hour, then a 3-mile-run that had to be completed at a seven-minute-mile pace. If you fail to complete two runs at that pace, you're automatically dropped from the course. Then you would have to report to your unit and stand in front of your soldiers without airborne wings, which meant you were either too scared to try or not tough enough to finish.

After injuring my knee, I fell back on one of the runs and had to take 5 days of medical leave and then recycle. I spent the five days icing my knee and doing PT and then started the second week over again. I made it through the first few runs of week two when my knee started to bother me again, and I fell out of another run. I was called into the Sergeant Major's office and given the news once again. If I continued with this class and fell out of one more run I would be dropped from the course. If I chose to recycle, I would have the rest of the week off from training and then could begin week two all over again. It was time to ask myself a very difficult question. "How badly do I really want this?". The answer came back quickly. I want this with every fiber of my being! I spent the rest of the week as the night duty officer and had my days to myself. I made good use of the time resting and running during the day and catching a few hours of sleep. I began week two once again and the 3rd time was a charm. I was ready for jump week!

To earn your wings, you must successfully complete five jumps. This meant landing on the drop zone, gathering your parachute, and running off the drop zone under your own power. Any injury that required assistance would mean automatic failure. Failure was not an option. After I landed my fifth jump, two of my Fordham classmates, who were at Ft. Benning, waiting to start Ranger School, showed up to pin on my jump wings. I was thrilled to see my two old buddies for a quick visit and a welcome into the Fraternity of Paratroopers.

The fire in my belly that brought me to ROTC, and later to compete for and win an active duty commission, also inspired me to stick it out at Airborne school. There was simply no way I was leaving Fort Benning without those Airborne wings. As I look back on it now, even though it was all a grind, none of it felt like work. My passion for what I was doing was intense. My refusal to accept rejection was proving to become a pattern in my life. Maybe more than a pattern, it was becoming an ethos. No matter what, I would never quit.

Go West Young Man!

My first duty station was Fort Lewis in Tacoma, Washington. Originally the plan after I completed Airborne School was to return to New York and pick up my brother Jim. The two of us planned to enjoy a great road trip across the northern United States from New York to Tacoma, Washington. Unfortunately, my delays at Airborne School made it impossible for Jim to accompany me on the trip. Instead, I bought Jim a round-trip ticket to Ireland for the week he had taken off work.

Leaving New York meant leaving everything behind. I was leaving my family and friends. I was leaving behind my life as a New York Irish musician. I was also leaving behind the possibility of a long-term relationship with a former high school girlfriend from Stony Point with whom I had reconnected when I was in Virginia.

Immediately after Airborne School, I returned to New York for a quick five-day leave to say farewell to family and friends. During my time home, I had the thrill of watching my younger brother John, a junior at West Point, box in the Brigade Championship. Later that night, I packed up my belongings for my 2900 mile trip to Ft. Lewis, WA, which included, courtesy of my Irish Catholic mother, the comforter from my boyhood twin bed. Message sent and received.

Making the crossing from New York to Tacoma required more courage than jumping out of airplanes. I believe the crossing truly required courage because I did not know what was waiting on the other side. The Pacific Northwest may have been another planet for all I knew. My little Chevy Cavalier took me through New York, Pennsylvania, Ohio, Illinois, Indiana, Minnesota, South Dakota, Montana, Idaho and finally into the state of Washington. I drove 2900 miles in 5 days. It took me until seeing Mount Rushmore in Rapid City, South Dakota to figure out that I was on the adventure of a lifetime. I was boldly going where no Keenan had gone before! America, even the small towns and desolate prairies, was so beautiful it's difficult to find the words to describe it.

I had made my commitment and was duty and honor bound to see it through and to serve as best I could. When you want something badly enough, you will sacrifice nearly everything to achieve it. By gaining the active duty commission, I had achieved my goal but sacrificed my life in New York. At the time, I seriously considered proposing marriage to my love interest in New York. When I discussed the possibility of a long-distance relationship, she rejected the idea. Because I could not see the possibility of marriage for some time to come, we sadly parted ways. Life boils down to a few critical moments and we have to live with the choices we make in those moments.

Life in the Top Left Corner

On a cold rainy morning in early March, I signed into 3rd Battalion, 9th Aviation Regiment. No, I'm not a helicopter pilot. My branch was supply and logistics and that specialty was needed in every unit throughout the Army. The Officers were gathered outside headquarters and they were all stretching before PT (physical training). I found a place in the circle and everyone stretched down to their left foot and when I did, the man next to me reached down and untied my right shoelace. I thought nothing of it, re-tied my shoelace and then we stretched again, and the same man untied my shoelace. All of the other officers saw what was going on and I could hear them chuckling amongst themselves. I stood straight up, got right in his face and said, "Your name wouldn't happen to be Dick, would it?" I saw a smile start to form on his face and then he broke out in a loud belly laugh, and all of the other officers were howling. This was my introduction to First Lieutenant Scott Padgett.

Scott 'Scooter' Padgett became my mentor whose first lesson was to inform me that, as a brand new Second Lieutenant, I knew nothing. I followed him for the first few weeks and watched how he interacted with his soldiers. I could not have found a better role model. He genuinely cared for his soldiers and his first priority was that they had everything they needed to achieve their mission. Scott also imparted another piece of wisdom. He told me to seek out the most physically fit of my soldiers and to make sure that I scored one point higher on the physical fitness test than that soldier. To the troops, actions spoke louder than words.

During my two years in the Pacific Northwest (PNW), I spent my weekends traveling from Vancouver down to Los Angeles and all points in-between. I spent many nights running around the city of Seattle with a stellar crew of bachelor Lieutenants seeking interaction with the fairer gender. This was an incredibly happy period in my life. I went to work every day with my best friends. With these same friends I visited places I could never have imagined. I started to feel that there was no place in the world where I couldn't feel comfortable.

During Operation Desert Shield, we learned that our unit was not going to deploy. Every few days I would get a phone call from a friend telling me that they were headed to the Gulf. I went to my commanding officer and requested an assignment to a unit that was deploying to the Gulf. LTC Hirsch sat me down and gave me some fatherly advice. He had flown helicopters in Vietnam and had seen more than his fair share of war. He said "Billy, don't be in a hurry. If this war lasts six months we're all going to have to go anyway." He also reminded me that I was working in a position normally held by a Major. In other words, I was holding down a job two ranks ahead of mine. Lt. Colonel Hirsch had afforded me a tremendous opportunity. I had such respect for my commander that I accepted his advice and did not protest his denial of my request for a transfer. An overseas deployment would have to wait for the time being. While I didn't deploy to the Persian Gulf, many helicopter pilots from Fort Lewis were sent to the Gulf. This proved to be a lucky break for young Lieut. Keenan!

As a bachelor officer, the Army added a few hundred dollars into my check to pay for living quarters. My living quarters just happened to be a three bedroom house on American Lake. I shared the house with two captains John and Randy who were helicopter pilots. Our rent was so cheap that we bought a small motorboat so we could waterski! Life in the lake house was a time of "work hard and play harder". We hosted epic parties, made a lot of new friends, and had endless amounts of fun. Such was life in the top left corner. I loved every minute of it.

Two years at Fort Lewis took me from a 22-year-old college grad to an accomplished 24-year-old First Lieutenant who had served as a platoon leader, company executive officer, junior staff officer, and Battalion Operations Officer. I had learned my craft and was ready for higher levels of command. From Scott Pagett and LTC Hirsch, I learned the importance of the role of a mentor. Because I had greatly benefited from their counsel, I was able to become the same kind of leader to the soldiers under my command.

From my travels I learned there is a great big world out there and I wanted to experience as much of it as I could. I fell in love with our country all over again. I had seen the desolate prairie, the majestic Mt. Rainier, and the beautiful beaches of Waikiki. I began my journey on active duty in the fall of 1989, and by the fall of 1991, I started asking myself, "what's next?"

CHAPTER 3

CHANGES IN LATITUDES, CHANGES IN ATTITUDES

I was out with a bunch of my buddies and expressed to them my desire to do a "hardship tour", which is usually overseas, and in Spartan living conditions. Once again, I was pursuing my old friend "deliberate discomfort". My two choices were Korea for a full year or a little known 6-month tour of duty in the Republic of Honduras where I would live in a "hooch". I chose Honduras. There were several major advantages of going to Honduras. First, after two rain soaked years in the Pacific Northwest (PNW) I would be spending 180 days in the tropics, with constant sunshine and high temperatures! Secondly, the tour of duty in Honduras was considered temporary duty (TDY) which entitled me to an additional $18 a day. This would prove to be a financial boon as there was almost nowhere to spend my money. Third, the mission of our unit in Honduras was to implement the US foreign-policy of "low intensity conflict". At first I did not understand what the term "low intensity conflict" meant. As the deployment drew nearer, I came to understand the mission. A "high intensity conflict" would be a "shooting war". A "low intensity conflict" was a Cold War. I had been under the impression that the Cold War ended in 1989. We would be out in the Honduran countryside winning the hearts and minds of the Hondurans so they would not resort to a single party

Marxist dictatorship. I would be working to keep communism out of our hemisphere. This was a real world mission!

I took a two week leave over the Christmas holiday to spend time with family and friends before leaving for Honduras. The absolute last thing I wanted was any romantic entanglement. On the evening of December 27th, 1991, my best friend Michael and I went to a bar called Jeremiah's in New City for a few beers. There was a group of girls in the bar and gradually Michael and I drifted over and started chatting them up. There was one cute petite blonde who caught my eye. The two of us huddled together apart from the rest of the group and then I asked her name. She was a cousin of my next door neighbor in Stony Point whom I knew since the age of eight when my Dad and I would play music at their family parties. Back then she was just a child of four years old, and now I was 24 and she was 20. At the end of the night she jumped in, the front seat of my car, and we dropped off Michael. Instead of driving her home she directed me to a local makeout spot. Prior to this I did not believe in love at first sight. After taking her home at 3AM, I took out my journal and wrote these words, "Tonight I met the girl I'm going to marry."

Sara and I spent every minute of my leave together, and then It was time to go. I wanted to be fair and offered her the chance to see other people while I was gone, but we both agreed to just see each other. That very special young lady would become the recipient of 180 letters, one letter posted for each day that I was gone.

In January 1992, I left the rainy and cold PNW and flew to Charleston, South Carolina. After a long night of sleeping on the floor in an Air Force base, I boarded a C-5 Galaxy for the final leg of the journey. I landed in Honduras and was picked up at the flight line in a Willys Jeep that looked like something from the TV show MASH. The lieutenant who picked me up was very happy to see me because I was his replacement. He drove me to my new quarters which was a wooden hut with screens for windows and a corrugated tin roof. These huts were called hooches. I stowed my duffle bag, suitcase, and guitar in my hooch, changed into a pair of shorts and was immediately taken to a BBQ.

In Honduras, the work week was from Monday through Friday 7 AM - 5 PM and Saturdays 7 AM - 12 noon. This first party that I attended had as its featured attraction a roast pig prepared by two Samoan soldiers who dug a pit and roasted it island style. Within my first hour of being in Honduras, I was in shorts, a t-shirt, flip flops, eating a plate of pork, rice, and beans, and had a cold beer in my hand. "Bill," I thought to myself, "you made a great decision."

I took up my duties as an Executive Officer, second in command to a Captain. Two weeks into my tour, my Commander fell ill and as a 24 year old First Lieutenant, I was suddenly thrust into command. My superiors told me that they would find a Captain to fill the slot within a few weeks. I had other plans. My plan was to do such a good job that it would be impossible for them to take the command away from me. After one month, my battalion commander summoned me to his office and said "Bill you haven't cocked it up too badly, so I'm going to let you command." This incredible opportunity put me at least three years ahead of my peer group and would have easily set me up for rapid promotion.

Life in Honduras was a complete blast. When we weren't working, we were partying. Together with another company commander, I started to perform music every Tuesday night. Andy Seward and I set up a small PA, two microphones, two guitars, and played songs by the Beatles, Eagles, Garth Brooks, Jimmy Buffett, etc. The Bill and Andy show became a huge hit and we were paid $50 a piece which was beer money for the remainder of the week.

In July 1992, with my command coming to end, I had to make my decision to continue in the Army or to come home. My command slot as a First Lieutenant had catapulted me at least two years past my peer group. Most lieutenants commissioned in 1989 would have to wait until promotion to captain in order to become a company commander. My path to rapid promotion was paved for me and I gave it serious consideration. My time in Honduras resulted in my falling in love with our country all over again. The desperate poverty I had witnessed in my travels in Central America gave me a completely new appreciation for all that we have in the US. If I had stayed in the Army, I would have immediately deployed to Somalia in East Africa. I had been away long enough. It was time to come home. This decision came straight from the heart. I had missed too many weddings, Christmases, and wakes. I missed my family. I missed New York and playing Irish music. Above all, I missed the girl I had met on December 27th, 1991.

On the very date that I was supposed to leave Honduras I caught a lucky break. The Commanding General of the New Jersey National Guard had been in Honduras for training and was due to leave on the very same day that I was. He offered me a ride home on the plane that he was sharing with three of his other officers. We flew directly from Honduras to an airbase in South Jersey and I picked up a rental car and drove straight to see Sara. When I came into the house she was waiting for me on the couch and her mother had hung a banner that said "Welcome Home, Billy". I didn't understand why she didn't get up and come running up the stairs to greet me. She just sat there looking beautiful and waiting for me to come down to her. Many years later, I realized that she thought a marriage proposal was imminent. This was a "critical moment" in life when everything was right and I did not act, believing there was so much time.

My brother John, a graduate of West Point class of 1991, was getting married at the Academy on July 20th of 1992. It was a beautiful evening and my girlfriend and I did not miss a single dance the whole night. After the wedding my parents and Sara and I went for a week's vacation in Ocean City, New Jersey. My leave flew by and it was time to return to Fort Lewis for my final three months in the Army. I moved right back into my room at the lake house and the good times resumed as if I had never left. On Saturdays I began classes for my transition to civilian life. I set my sights on securing a job as a pharmaceutical sales rep. My cousin Michael, a former Marine, had transitioned successfully into pharmaceutical sales and as I admired him greatly I thought that this would be a career for me. The truth is I had no idea what a pharma sales rep did except that the job brought with it a generous salary, bonuses, and a company car. Many of the top companies sought Junior Military Officers (JMOs-Lieutenants and Captains) and used corporate headhunters to find suitable candidates.

My final day in the Army was in October 1992. Rather than take the fastest way home across I-90 and the northern states, I decided to get lost in America for a few weeks. My dear old Dad signed me up for AAA just before I departed the PNW and I received a "Trip Ticket" which was a flip up book with a yellow line marking the roads that I should travel and a red star for my destination. Every other day I would stop and spend time with great friends in San Francisco, Monterrey, and my mom's sister Peg (A Catholic nun) at Loyola Marymount University in Los Angeles. I had my own room in the convent and every morning I would have breakfast with the Sisters before picking up a six-pack of beer and driving to the beach. In the evenings my Aunt Peg and I would get together for dinner in Marina del Rey where she treated me to a great Mexican dinner and a frozen Margarita, no salt. Driving out of L.A. my next destination was Phoenix, Arizona. I pulled onto Interstate 10 for the straight shot across the desert, rolled all the windows down, and put on a cassette copy of Bruce Springsteen Live 1975-1985. I wanted to see what my Honda Accord could do, so I put it into fifth gear and hit 90 mph. It was a total rush of freedom as I heard the words "Promised Land". I had reached California, made a hard left. While this is three months later, and headed east to that beautiful girl I left behind.

There were so many memorable experiences during this wonderful time of getting lost in America, but one of the most poignant happened when I least expected it. I pulled into Memphis, TN and drove straight to Graceland. I boarded a bus with what seemed like 40 people from the Far East, each loaded with high speed cameras, and I was armed only with my One-time-use box camera. At the end of the tour everyone gathered at Elvis' gravesite. There were literally hundreds of people gathered around and the song "Love Me Tender" was being piped in by speakers located around the property. People all around me were crying and holding onto each other for support. I had never been a huge fan of Elvis except for his 1968 comeback special when he wore black leather and turned in what I consider to be his greatest performance. I never would have expected it, but I got caught up in the emotion and found myself with tears running down my cheeks. I felt a wave of sadness come over me thinking he was only 40 when he met his maker. Elvis had so much more to give. If he could have gotten clean, imagine the music that he had left in him. My morning at Graceland taught me to make the most of every day.

After crying with "The King " I spent the night in Savannah, Georgia with Scott Padgett and his family. Scott was doing his company command tour. I pulled out of Savannah the next morning at 5 AM and drove 17 hours straight to get home. There was a girl waiting for me and I had been away long enough. I arrived at my parents house at 11 PM and had a true Forrest Gump moment. When I opened the front door, Mom and Dad were already in bed and I said, "Momma, I'm home".

Lessons Learned the Hard Way

The morning after I arrived home, I woke up early and drove to my old barber and got a good haircut. During my three-week sojourn across America, I let my hair grow for the first time in nearly four years. Once out of the barber's chair, I made a beeline for my girlfriend's house. It would be difficult to put into words the joy that I felt the first moment I saw her and knew that we would be together as a couple without thousands of miles separating us. She was in her senior year at a nearby college. I was living with my parents and going to job interviews several times a week. To bring in extra money, I rejoined my old band from my college days.

It never occurred to me that the transition of military to civilian life could be very difficult. Back at home I realized how much I missed my buddies. I missed a world where everything made sense.

In a mad rush to begin my civilian life, I used corporate recruiters to set up interviews. For the first and only time in my life, I took a job strictly for the money. I believed that my experience and record of success had prepared me for life in the corporate world. Junior Military Officers were a hot commodity and I set my sight on going into pharmaceutical sales. I was hired by the number one pharmaceutical company in the world. The problem was that I hadn't considered what my day to day life would be like. As a Pharmaceutical Sales Representative (PSR) I was given a company car, samples of the medications, and a list of doctors who I had to convince to prescribe my company's medications. Each day in the Army, I went to work with all of my best buddies. Now I was in a car for 8-10 hours a day, by myself, going from office to office. More often than not, I would wait 45 minutes to an hour to speak with a doctor, only to be given 30 seconds of his or her time. All they wanted were my samples and to know when I could bring in lunch for the whole office.

I always thought of myself as someone who could get along with anyone, that is, until I met my boss. Peter was sarcastic, lacked personality, and looked to trip you up at any opportunity. The worst part of it was that he insisted that I move into an apartment in my sales territory rather than living at home in Rockland. He was right in that my territory began a 40 minute drive from my house, but I left the Army so I could be home for a while. Just like any bad relationship, it was wrong from the start, and I stayed longer than I should have.

I stayed in this awful job for 18 months because I was afraid to quit, afraid to be viewed as a failure in the eyes of my Mom and Dad. My unwillingness to ask for help would have disastrous consequences. The uncertainty in my professional life bled over into my personal life, causing me to make relationship decisions that I would later live to regret.

Post Army Dating Life

I left the Army for Sara. She was a great girl from a great family. Everyone in both of our families were delighted that we were together. During the time we were together there was a genuine love story. I have a lifetime of memories. My dissatisfaction in my work led me to becoming emotionally unavailable for her when she was going through a tough time. Rather than stay with her and help her through it, I stepped back. I cannot help but think that if I were happy in my work, the outcome would have been vastly different.

After Sara, there was Debbie. We shared a great many common interests and she absolutely loved my music. Many of our dates included running, trips to Connecticut to spend time with her large family, and time in her apartment in Yonkers. Many times before going to sleep, she would put my guitar in my lap and ask me to sing to her. Our relationship would become another casualty courtesy of the pharmaceutical industry and my dissatisfaction with my life and with myself.

Then there was Shannon. We met when I was out playing in a bar in New Jersey. After the show, she came up to the stage with a group of friends and we immediately hit it off. I showed her my brand new guitar and she acted genuinely impressed. Shannon and I golfed together, played one-on-one basketball together, and enjoyed a very passionate romantic life together. We would attend Sunday Mass at her parish and at the "handshake of peace", she would kiss my cheek and whisper, "Billy, this is the church we are going to get married in." I could not have agreed more. Many of her friends were getting married during our time together. I know she was waiting for me to propose. My angst in my work life kept me from proposing. I told her that I had decided to leave the company I was working for before I told my parents. I have no doubt that she knew that this would only delay the engagement. I put unnatural pressure on myself that everything had to be perfect for me to propose. People all around the world get engaged without having any clue what they're going to do to pay the bills. Somehow, these rules did not apply to me.

I remember well when the day arrived that I broke the news to my parents. We went to Mass and then out to a diner to get a bite to eat for breakfast. Over breakfast I told them, "I'm quitting my job." Their responses were not unexpected.

"What are you doing? Have you lost your mind? That's a great job! What are you going to do now? Are you having a nervous breakdown?" I looked across the table and told them that my mind was made up and nothing could change the decision. I was not going to be miserable for the rest of my life, just for the money.

My hard-working parents, children of Irish immigrants, grew up in the Bronx. Their version of the American Dream was that each new generation of our family would climb up another rung of the ladder. My job included a great salary, a large bonus, a company car, and an expense account. I wore tailored suits, wing tipped shoes, and played the part of a successful salesman. For several years camouflage and combat boots fit perfectly. No matter how hard I tried, the tailored suit never fit. The problem was that I was living to work instead of working to live a life. I needed to break free.

My rush to begin my civilian life caused me to neglect to ask myself the most important question: Which career path would enable me to have the same passion that I had in the military? What I did not count on was the feeling of disconnectedness upon leaving the Army. Being part of a team, the work, and camaraderie that were integral to my military experience were no longer present in my life. I needed a career in the civilian world that would give me the same sense of purpose.

I loved serving my country and going to work every day with my best friends, but I believe I left for the right reasons. I missed my parents and my friends. I missed the music on the New York Irish circuit. More than anything, I missed Sara. As I look back on my life, I think she really was "the one".

CHAPTER 4

SOUL SEARCH
IN THE OLD COUNTRY

Summer 1994. Far from having a nervous breakdown, I was having a nervous breakthrough. I had gone straight from company command to pharmaceutical sales without really taking the time to think about a career that would bring me happiness. I also knew that being single without children, I had the opportunity to take a breath and find myself. I decided to return to that place where I had found myself so many years ago. Ireland was calling me back. Luckily, I didn't have to make the trip by myself. My travel companion was a 55-year-old retired NYPD Detective, accordion player, and singer—my dad.

We spent three weeks in Ireland playing music, drinking pints, and taking long drives in between stops. Our very first stop was in a little town called Doolin in West Clare. Doolin is a place that boasts some of Ireland's best musicians and singers. We pulled into town, checked into our Bed and Breakfast (B&B) in the early afternoon, and walked into a pub called McDermott's. I left my instruments back in our room because I didn't know if I would be welcomed into the circle of musicians. Dad and I got a table in the pub and started drinking. One by one, the musicians started to trickle in and take their place on the stage. There was a flute, a banjo, a bouzouki, and a 1963 Hofner violin bass (like Paul McCartney's) played by a 65 year old above- the-knee-amputee named Teddy McCormick. The tunes were fabulous but to our disappointment there was no singing.

After an hour, I had to go to the bathroom and when I came back, Dad had worked his magic. He told the musicians that I was a great guitarist and singer, and I was being beckoned onto the stage. I sat on a bar stool and a guitar was handed to me, already plugged into the PA system. I asked the audience, "Does anyone have a request?" An old man shouted, "The Isle of Innisfree." This was a song I had sung for years. I belted it out and the place went absolutely mad. I turned around and handed the guitar back to the band. They handed it back to me and asked me to sit down and sing more songs. The audience was going bonkers.

"Tell them who you are and where you are from," the bandleader said. After 18 months of feeling completely lost and disconnected, I had to fly 3,000 miles and drive to this little seaside town to find myself. One song and the smile on my father's face put me back on the path to realizing who I really was. It was a good first step.

I leaned into the microphone. "Hi everyone, I am Billy Keenan and I am from New York." Hearing this, the crowd went even more wild. This was the first day of our trip and my soul search. I had felt that I was letting my father down by quitting a good-paying job but on the first day in Ireland, when I looked down from the stage, all I saw was a gleaming smile of pride.

We spent a lot of time with family and everywhere I went I pulled out the guitar and started playing and singing. Rarely did we ever have to pay for a pint of beer. On one of the longer drives, the barriers that exist naturally between father and son started to disappear and I felt like I was talking to one of my buddies. My dad actually asked me about the girl I was dating. He asked "does she enjoy the physical side of romance?". I started to laugh and said "Dad, there's no worries in that department."

Dad and I had reunited with the New York Leitrim society and we were staying in Kelly's Hotel in the town of Mohill. We were tired from the road trip and took a long nap. Upon waking, we both freshened up and headed downstairs looking for food and drink. Arriving at the bar, we quickly found out that it was karaoke night and the grand prize was 50 pounds. I had no intention of entering the contest. Dad, however, kept egging me on saying "Go on, go on, you have to enter." I argued that being a professional, it wasn't fair. Let these amateurs have their fun, but he still kept at it until I signed up for the contest. There were many great singers but one man was the local favorite, and his party piece was "Friends in Low Places "by Garth Brooks. I was up after him and my selection was "Only the Lonely" by Roy Orbison. I sang the song perfectly, and at the end of the last verse, when Roy goes into his third octave, I sang in falsetto. I hit the note perfectly, and the room sat in stunned silence. I had defeated the local hero, graciously accepted the 50 pound prize, and dad and I had another free night of drinks. I don't know if I ever saw him smiling and laughing more.

This time in my life taught me many things, but the most important was that it's okay to not have all the answers in every moment.

My best friend Michael got married in October 1995. I had just broken up with Shannon in July, and I was back in school to get my teaching certification. I was living the life of a full-time student at the age of 27, supporting myself by playing music every weekend. I'd spent the summer playing midweek gigs at a place in East Durham with two of my best friends, Brendan O'Sullivan and Jimmy Kelly. The gigs were phenomenal and we attracted a following of young girls everywhere we went. I was young, single, and ready to mingle, and I had my mojo back! School was a breeze, and I felt that I was truly on the right path.

Shortly after I had begun my life as a full time student, I attempted to rekindle my relationship with Sara. We had one magical night out dancing at a pub in Yonkers, and I thought she was mine once again. After a desperate week of phone calls, she finally answered and said "I'm sorry, but I have decided to go back to my old boyfriend". I was devastated and even with this disappointment, I continued to search for lasting love. I made the mistake of trying to reconnect with Debbie, only to find her already seeing someone, and once again I faced rejection.

Undeterred, I was still so happy in my coursework that I continued to look for the last piece in the calculus of happiness. In my coursework at RCC, there were two Irish girls, Oona and Nuala, whom I had befriended and spent many a pleasant afternoon with after school. Oona was the co-owner of the Claddagh Hotel & Restaurant with her ex-boyfriend. Of the two, I had fallen for Oona, hook, line and sinker. One Saturday night on the way back from a wedding, I stopped in to see Oona at the restaurant for a late night session. Just before leaving, I told her of my feelings for her and asked her to go out with me. She told me she could not, because Nuala had fallen for me. This rejection did not stop me from looking for love, but led me to lower my standards and expectations. One of my best friends in the Army had a great phrase that I had simply forgotten "I'd rather be alone than keep bad company".

My brother John and his wife Denise had just welcomed their second daughter into the world, and the Christening was held at the Blauvelt Irish Center in January. I popped in for a few hours and joined Peter McKiernan and Brendan O'Sullivan for a few tunes.

As I was on my way out, I caught the eye of a girl named Anne. She was a few years younger than me and looked good, and I filed that in the back of my mind.

I slept in the next day, having played a late gig the night before, and found Anne's number. Anne and I agreed to go out on Thursday night. I picked her up at her apartment down on 84th St. in Yorkville and we headed north to Yonkers to a restaurant called Tara's on Midland Avenue. Dermot Henry played every Thursday night and I knew it was always a great place to go for a quiet pint and a few laughs with Dermot. We had a great time and enjoyed the conversation and the music. I took her back to her place where we hugged and had a little peck on the cheek, and agreed to meet up again the following weekend. We had another date, another great time, and as I walked her up to her apartment she turned the key, opened the door, invited me in, and we made out. I said good night and started to leave and she invited me to stay. I thought to myself "Hey now! Maybe I do still have the mojo!". We walked back to her room and started to get ready for bed. We got under the covers on her futon and I made my move. Nothing too dramatic, just a gradual inching over to her side of the bed for a little spooning. She stopped my advance saying something about being tired. So I'm thinking to myself, "What the hell did she ask me to stay for?". I rolled over and went to sleep thinking things would get rolling, just give it some time. Four months later, we were in the middle of a great relationship in every way conceivable except one, physical intimacy. Beyond making out, there was nothing.

My self-esteem was beaten to death. Between the debacle with Sarah, chasing after Debbie, Mike's wedding, and now Anne's disinterest in engaging in a physical romantic relationship, I was in the danger zone. At this point, I think it is of the utmost importance to address "the honest conversation". In my post-Army dating life, if I had had an honest conversation with any of the wonderful girls I had dated, the relationship could have been saved. Specifically with Anne, if I had only said "We don't have to make love, let's just lay here and face one another and kiss and hold each other." Maybe she just needed to hear that I loved her and that would have opened up the well of passion. My inability to have "the honest conversation" would lead me into peril that would impact the rest of my adult life in ways that I could never have imagined.

In April of 1996, my band was playing a gig at Mustang Harry's near Madison Square Garden in New York City. My girlfriend Anne came into the bar by herself and sat down at the bar for the first set. While we were going through the first set, a group of ten people came into the bar and I knew right away it was a wedding couple and their friends coming to check out our band. I led the band through a killer first set and after ninety minutes, we took our first break. I immediately went down off the stage to see Anne and spend a few moments with her before going to see the wedding couple. She said she was only going to stay for a few more minutes and then go home. I should have known it at the time, but just the fact that she showed up by herself meant she truly had strong feelings for me. She was just waiting for me to express my commitment to her, then I felt she would be open to physical intimacy. She left the bar and I got to work schmoozing Vincent and Geraldine who were coming to check out the band for their wedding. Just before we started the second set, my drummer pointed out Meghan who was going to be part of the wedding party and said "Billy, she would be a great girl for you."

To tell you the truth, of all the girls in the bar that night, I hadn't even noticed her. After the gig was over, he continued to extol her virtues, talking about how she was the bartender at a hotel in the Catskills and was lively, cute, and perky. I started asking questions and found out that she hung out in O'Malley's in Pearl River. One night on the way home from a wedding reception on a Sunday night, I stopped in. Having just broken things off with Anne, I was looking for her. Rather than let a loving relationship find me, I was pressing and went looking for it. I got up and played a few songs with the band and then spotted Meghan, sauntered over, and asked her to dance. After we danced, I asked her if I could buy her a drink. She said yes, and we walked over to the bar, only to be confronted by a big, Irish-born guy who had clearly set his sights on Meghan. I sensed what was going on and started to leave the bar, saying "OK, no problem." I started to walk out and Meghan followed me. We had a quick conversation and agreed to go out to dinner in a few days. At that first dinner date I did a lot of talking. I remember one of the first things she said was that she'd heard I had a big ego and she'd have to do something about that. I thought she was kidding. A few more dates and we went from a goodnight kiss in the car, to a goodnight kiss in the kitchen of her house, to a goodnight kiss in her bedroom. Then one night, we were out to hear another

Irish band, and we both got very drunk. We took a cab back to her house, went upstairs and that, as they say, was that. Thus began an intense physical relationship. As I look back on it now, there was no romance, just a physical act and release. In my mind at the time, all the rejection of the past year had been wiped away.

Physical intimacy came too quickly, before a deep personal relationship evolved, which was the thing that I was craving the most. But two months straight of physical intimacy had me emotionally drunk by the end of August. I never stopped to realize that all we ever did Monday to Friday was sit on her couch after she got home from work and then go to bed. I worked every weekend with the band while she was up in the Catskills bartending at a hotel. We never actually dated. I never noticed that she didn't have any other interest because I was too busy being happy. Besides, I was interested in everything. I was sure at some point there would be some common interest that we could engage in together. But it never happened.

I Should Have Known Better

I had been working at Albertus Magnus as an assistant soccer coach, while I was studying for my teaching certification. When I got the call from Albertus Magnus in August 1996 for a full-time social studies teaching position, I felt my life was taking shape. For the first time since leaving the Army, with my professional future secured, I felt I could get married. For the first 12 weeks of Fall semester, I should have been student teaching as part of the certification program at St. Thomas Aquinas College. I would have been paying tuition and teaching for free. Instead, the Education Department agreed to use my time at Albertus as my student teaching experience and granted my certification. I was getting paid and had medical benefits. If I had student-taught for free, I would never have been able to accumulate the $3,000 it took to purchase a diamond ring.

I began teaching in September of 1996. In addition to teaching, I coached Varsity soccer, directed the school play, served as the music minister at weekly liturgy, continued my Masters classes two days a week, and performed on the weekends. I absolutely loved teaching at Albertus! I had no time for a relationship. The only thing I had in common with Meghan was physical intimacy. My only dates with Meghan were sleeping over her house when her parents were 100 miles away in the Catskill Mountains. In what appears now to be a manic episode, I proposed on Thanksgiving Eve of 1996. We had only been dating for seven months. At the time, my father was recovering from thyroid cancer surgery and, when I showed him the ring I had bought, he summoned very little enthusiasm.

Throughout the whole summer leading up to my Dad's cancer surgery, I took refuge in Meghan's bed. Not once did I bring her to my parents house. Why didn't I bring her home? The reason is I was ashamed—not of her but of how I spent the whole summer in this girl's house night after night, and my parents knew that she was alone. Every other girl I had dated was like part of my family. Now I was getting engaged to a girl my parents had never met. As I look back on it now, this was clearly a sign that once again I had lost my way.

"What is your plan? How are you going to propose?" my Dad asked me. The answer was, I had no plan. I had the ring and it was burning a hole in my pocket. In addition to the ring, I bought a card and wrote out the promise, "We will always have everything we need, and most of what we want." That was my promise. That night after dinner, we went to the Nanuet Mall and walked around aimlessly. I brought her home and I was so nervous about proposing that I was silent on the drive to her house. She started to get annoyed with me, but as I walked her up to the door, I dropped to one knee and proposed.

As I look back on it now, my proposal spoke volumes about the relationship. I had no plan for a romantic proposal. In fact, it was devoid of all romance. When I dropped to one knee, her annoyance became joy. We went inside, told her parents, and her father brought out a bottle of Irish Whisky.

Buyer's Remorse

Almost immediately after proposing, I experienced buyer's remorse. The date Meghan chose for our wedding–the day after Thanksgiving 1997–I was already booked to play a wedding. When I informed her that the other wedding was non-negotiable because I had signed a contract and would be liable should I cancel, she was apoplectic. In addition to her anger at changing the date she was even more furious at Jim Cunningham of the Cunningham Brothers who would be playing at our wedding. The Cunningham Brothers played every wedding in the Keenan family, and their father was the bandleader at my parent's wedding reception in 1964. Jim and I had a long, happy, and very prosperous relationship.

After a few days of nonstop petulance from her, I took back the ring and broke off the engagement one month after proposing. After a week of phone calls from both her and her parents that I artfully avoided, she tried one more time. My Mom picked up the phone, thrusted it into my hands, and said "You have to talk to her." Meghan relented on the wedding date change and on the choice of band for the reception, but never once in that long conversation did I hear the words "I'm sorry" or "I love you." Her only concern was getting the ring back. I had given the ring to my Mom and said "No matter what I say, do not give this ring back to me." Now after the phone attacks, I was demanding the ring from my mother. Reluctantly, she gave it to me and, just like that, the engagement was back on.

In January, we attended pre-cana classes (a series of workshops in preparation for a Catholic marriage) at Immaculate Conception in Stony Point. On the way there we were talking excitedly about the wedding when out of nowhere Meghan got very quiet and said, "Don't say anything about taking back the ring." She said this in a deadly serious manner. My thinking was, "Isn't this the perfect time to talk about our differences and how we can work on making them better." Her answer was, "If you say you took back the ring, the moderator is going to think we should not get married." We went through the pre-cana sessions and I said nothing about taking back the ring. It was as if we had to cheat to get through the exam qualifying us to be married.

Obviously, something was wrong from the beginning. After all of the stress and turmoil over the band, the problem should have been put to rest. However, Meghan scheduled a trip to Florida during my mid-winter recess. We arrived in Ft. Laurderdale, checked into the Holiday Inn and for the next five days, I never made it to the beach. As I look back on it now, I was clearly breaking away and she used physical intimacy to get me back under control. I wanted so much for my choice of a bride to be correct that I did not see the manipulation. Like the biblical Samson, I let myself be controlled by my greatest weakness– sex–instead of love. Shortly after the Florida trip, the subject of the wedding band reared its ugly head again. I was shocked and infuriated to have to deal with this subject once again. We had a fierce argument in the living room of her parents' house. I demanded that she hand the ring back. She refused and I stood up and walked down the stairs and her mother stopped me in the kitchen saying, "You two can do whatever you want when you're down in Florida, but when you're in my house, you don't go up to the bedroom." This woman actually thought I was upstairs fooling around, when, in reality, I was in a darkened living room fighting for my future happiness. I stayed away a few days and the phone calls kept coming. She reluctantly agreed to allow the Cunningham band to play at the wedding. Eventually out of a sense of obligation--not love, I put the engagement back on. Truth be told, our marriage never should have happened.

With each passing day I began a "just friends" relationship with a female teacher. In the Spring semester we were asked to direct the school play together. She and I spent a lot of time together and did a lot of stress eating. One day after the play was over, she said, "Billy, we got fat together, now we're gonna get thin together, let's start walking." We started walking everyday after school at Rockland Lake. After a short time, our walks turned into runs. I could've gotten in shape in a myriad of ways, but I chose to spend my time with this girl. In truth, I always liked this girl. I thought she was pretty, smart, and funny but I had a fiancée. I remember the exact moment when I realized the depth of feeling I had for this young woman. I had to learn the song "Fields of Gold" by Sting for a wedding that weekend. I started to sing a few lines. She then told me the exact literary reference that Sting got the line from. I knew right there and then, that this was a girl I could talk to about anything and everything. But with Meghan, I had nothing in common. I was completely conflicted with my feelings for this girl and the obligation that I saw in my engagement. How could it be so easy and natural with this girl, but so hard and difficult with Meghan? All my feelings and actions were that of a man in love but I just stopped short of telling her. I convinced myself that she would not feel the same way. I was trying very hard to do the "right thing". The fact that I had to try with Megan was all the information I needed. Of course hindsight is always 20/20, so I soldiered on in the completely wrong relationship.

Six months before the wedding, with Meghan's parents back up in the Catskills, I had open access to her bedroom. However, I had no desire. I could recall times when I went to sleep over her house, staying fully clothed and not getting under the covers. I twice attempted to call off the engagement. The first time was from a payphone at the Blue Hill golf course. I had been playing every Monday night at Slattery's bar in Nyack and there were girls everywhere. Every Monday I had to fight my way out of conversations with beautiful girls, and my only defense was that I was engaged.

On the way home from one of these Monday sessions, my father tried to talk to me about my relationship with Meghan. He said, "Billy, you just don't seem happy; you're a great guy and you deserve to be happy." At this point, I expressed complete frustration saying "Dad, I can't talk about it." He pressed the matter further and I finally blurted out, "I don't know why I can't make her happy." A few days later, I got a call from Jack, one of my father's best friends who invited me out to play a round of golf at Blue Hill. We had a great time and in the cart he echoed my fathers words "Billy, you're a great guy. This girl is wrong for you." Once again, I turned it on myself. What was I doing wrong? Why didn't I feel as if she loved me? I called Meghan from the golf course and told her we had to stop the engagement. I said, "It is not supposed to be this hard." She asked me to come over and talk about it, and I agreed, wanting to act like a man and do it face-to-face. Jack offered to come with me, but I said that I could handle it. I was so wrong. Once again I allowed myself to be manipulated into continuing the engagement. In a life of very few regrets, my inability to break it off at this point is one of my deepest regrets. I truly believe that if I had the courage to break the engagement, my life would have turned out very differently. I deserved to be with a woman who shared common interests and loved me, like the girl I walked and ran with every day. The fact that I settled for this marriage is my fault. I paid a very heavy price. Wouldn't any girl have wondered, "Why would I want to marry this guy if he keeps trying to get out of it?"

In early August 1997, all of my friends suffered the terrible loss of Billy Villeto, a great guy and the son of an Irish musician we all knew. Billy died tragically in a car accident on a Friday night. On Monday, my fellow musicians and I performed at Slattery's in a state of shock and grief. We were asked by his parents to play the music at the funeral Mass. After the burial we all convened at a restaurant for the repast. Surrounded by friends, I poured out my heart about the troubles I was having with the engagement. The more I talked, the more convinced I became that I had to act. Billy's death was the catalyst that shook me into action. I stood up and, once again, went to the pay phone, calling Meghan saying, "We have to end this. This is wrong. It is not supposed to be this hard. Engagement is supposed to be the happiest of times and this is not a happy time." She asked me to come over and so I did. This was the worst mistake that I could have made. I arrived at her house and I was resolved to break off the engagement. I called her to come downstairs, but she summoned me to her bedroom. I walked up the stairs slowly, and stood in the doorway of her room. She asked me to sit down on the bed and I did. You can guess where this ended up. Why didn't I see it for what it was?

Towards the end of the summer, something happened within me that I still am at a loss to explain. Meghan and I were at an Irish Festival, and to my surprise my parents also attended. This was after she had brought me back under control after my last attempt to end the engagement. To my parents, we looked like a happy couple. That very night, I told my parents "I'm thinking of ending the engagement. Something just doesn't feel right". This time, they argued the other way. "You two seem like such a happy couple; she seems like a very nice girl." After trying so many times to get out of the engagement, I began to look at it with a sense of resignation. I could not see a way out. I did not embrace the fact that I was going to be married. I felt worn down and had no fight left in me.

While all of this was going on, my parents informed me that I would have to move out and get an apartment because my brother Jim, his wife, and his infant son would be moving into the Stony Point house. I found a great apartment on Central Highway, and with my few meager possessions, set up my first bachelor pad. I loved living in that apartment. At the time I was teaching at Albertus, taking classes towards my Masters Degree at night, and every Friday, Saturday, and Sunday playing gigs with my band the Summer Wind. I rarely saw Meghan and that was just fine. When I did see her it was all about planning the wedding day. I found myself getting caught up in the momentum of planning the wedding but not all the days that would come after. Amazingly, when I think back on it, here I was in my own apartment, and she only came up one time. In September she said, "Let's hold off on having sex until the wedding night." Although I felt as if she was trying to control me, I was just fine with it. It was during this time that if I were living at home I could have spoken to my father about things. I needed to be saved and I was unable to do it myself.

Time to Face the Music

December 13th of 1997, I woke up showered, shaved, and put on a tuxedo. In the early afternoon, my brothers came by in a white limousine to pick me up. We drank a few beers on our way to the church. When I walked back into the sacristy I said hello to Father George and he turned to my brother and said, "The groom needs a breath mint." Before the wedding Mass, I walked around the church, shaking hands, hugging, and talking with people. One memory that sticks out in my mind is of the girl that I spent my engagement jogging with, who said, "You look great Billy, black is very slimming." After Meghan and I exchanged vows, I went to the lectern, picked up my guitar, and sang a song called "The Voyage". The song talks about working together, sitting out the doldrums and the storms, and still remaining in love. I made a great show that day, but the truth was that we had never worked together to resolve our problems. I should have seen that this marriage was wrong from the start and bound for disaster. The song's lyrics were wishful thinking on my part.

The Cunningham Brothers played at the reception. For our first dance I tried to consult Meghan but she couldn't come up with any suggestions. I chose Louis Armstrong's "Wonderful World". We did not make love the night of our wedding, but rather the next morning. I thought that this was a little bit strange, but truth be told it didn't bother me that much. We checked out of the Pearl River Hilton, got in my car, and, without thinking, I started to drive to her parents' house to drop her off. Then, I realized that I had to take her back to my apartment in Stony Point because I was married to her. I had one more week to teach before Christmas break, and then we were going to St. Thomas in the US Virgin Islands for our honeymoon. The first night we stayed in my apartment she complained because my bed was full size instead of a queen. I had purchased the bed while I was a single Army officer. None of the other women who had spent a night in that bed ever complained. When I came home from school on Monday after the wedding, I found my full size mattress and box spring in the hallway and a new queen size bed in the bedroom.

After opening all of the wedding gifts, we had a significant amount of money. I ran into a high school classmate at a bar in Rockland shortly after the wedding and he asked if I was looking for a house. My friend John was doing real estate part-time and said he'd found a great foreclosure in New City, New York. I said that I was interested and went to take a look. The house on Little Brook Lane was a large high ranch with 2600' sq. ft., five bedrooms, three bathrooms, and two fireplaces. The house sat on 6/10 of an acre and featured an in-ground pool in the backyard. I was a little hesitant to jump into a house because I was still working at a Catholic high school, but my in-laws urged us to buy the house.

There were six other potential buyers bidding for the house and in the middle of February, we found out that our bid was accepted. I was excited and looked forward to moving into the house but was told by my in-laws that it needed a good bit of work. Without being consulted, I was told that Meghan and I would be moving into my in-laws house to save money until the renovations could be completed. This was less than two months after the wedding. It's pretty difficult to get things going with your wife when her parents are asleep 30 feet away in the master bedroom.

We moved into our first house in the middle of March 1998. This was the busiest time of the year for my band Summerwind. From the beginning of the month, we were playing Irish dinner dances every Friday, Saturday and Sunday, and on St. Patrick's Day we played two gigs. It turned out that in order to pay my mortgage, I had to play gigs every weekend.

Luckily my classroom at Albertus was directly across the hall from the nurse's office. The school nurse knew of my double life and took pity on me. During my free period, she closed her office and let me sleep on one of the cots and gently woke me when it was time to go back and teach. It never occurred to me during this time that Meghan and I never did anything as a couple. We were newlyweds with absolutely nothing in common. The first year of our marriage, everything was about the house. I continued working at a blistering pace, never paying any mind to the shortcomings of our relationship. At the end of my first year at Albertus I realized that I would have to make a move to the public schools before I got too comfortable. Albertus is the kind of place where a teacher can become very comfortable. It is an incredible gift to be able to stop a lesson and talk about our faith in Jesus Christ. The kids did their homework and the parents were all involved. My salary at Albertus was $23,500. I was making $40,000 per year playing music. But if I wanted to start a family, I had to make a move.

I began looking in earnest for a public school position during my second year at Albertus. I went on several interviews and second interviews, but I received no offers. I returned for my third year, resolved and determined to secure a public school teaching position by the end of that year. In May 1999 I interviewed at North Rockland high school, taught a demonstration lesson, and got a job offer! In September 1999, I began a new chapter in my life as an educator. My first year salary nearly doubled my Albertus salary and I was enrolled in the New York State teachers retirement system. My future was secure! We began to talk about starting a family.

---------------------- CHAPTER 5 ----------------------

CARPE DIEM SURFING

By 2003 I had been married for six years, had two sons, Kieran and Patrick, born sixteen months apart, and two jobs. Patrick was born in July of 2000 and when he was only 8 months old, to my great surprise I found out we were expecting Kieran. On the weekends, Meghan worked part-time as a nurse, while I was available to watch the boys, before I played with the band at night. I was exhausted. I had let go of my disciplined physical fitness training by 2002 and was 60 pounds heavier then I was 10 years before when I left the military. In July 2003, we were at my parents' condo in Ocean City, New Jersey and I saw my Father sitting on the couch, holding my son Kieran, and growing weaker and weaker. Dad was in the last year of his struggle with thyroid cancer. As I looked at my Dad, I heard the voice of Robin Williams in his role as Mr. Keating in *Dead Poets Society*. Mr. Keating said the words, "carpe diem" to his students. Seize the day!

Out of nowhere, I jumped up and said "I'm going to the boardwalk to learn surfing." I drove up to the Seventh Street surf shop on the boardwalk, plunked down my $40, squeezed my chubby ass into a wetsuit, and waddled down to the water carrying a massive 10 foot longboard. In a class of nine and 10 year olds, I looked like Buddy the Elf. Once we got out in the ocean, the surf instructors pushed us into waves, telling us when to pop up. I had let myself get so out of shape that I could barely get to my feet. However, I did manage to catch one great wave, and I was absolutely hooked. Love at first sight. On the way home from the shore, I weighed myself at a rest stop. I had ballooned up from 160lbs. to 224 lbs. I immediately went on the Atkins diet and within six months I had lost 40 lbs. and rededicated myself to a life of fitness.

The cracks in our marriage began to show, usually over spending money. My wife was an extremely frugal woman. Throughout our marriage I would turn over all the money I made playing music to her, with the exception of twenty bucks for coffee during my work week. That's all I kept for myself. I never even had an ATM debit card. When she opened a bank account, she only got a card for herself. So when I needed a new piece of equipment I'd have to go to her for money, like a child. It never occurred to me to take control of, at least, the music money, which would have given me some power in the relationship. She looked at my instruments as toys rather than the tools of my trade. One night after she rejected my request to purchase a new instrument, in frustration and anger, I punched a hole in the closet door, which remained for the duration of our time in the house. I was not the type to physically lash out at anything, but my instruments were more than toys to me When I was alone in the house, I would take out my guitar and play songs that were the expression of emotions that I held secretly in my heart. Usually these songs evoked memories of the girls that I foolishly let slip through my fingers. For one of them, it was the song "I Will Whisper Her Name." For another, it was "The First Time Ever I Saw Your Face." My Mom's Aunt Anna passed away and the family wanted me to have her beautiful upright piano. When my wife and the boys were not home, I would sit at the piano and sing the song "God Only Knows" by the Beach Boys, remembering yet another old flame.

The house we had on Little Brook Lane was absolutely perfect. It had five bedrooms, a fully finished basement, and a half-acre backyard with an in-ground pool. I returned home from work one day to find out that Meghan wanted to move out of this house because the driveway was on a hill and the boys had ridden their big wheels out into the street. She wanted to move to a cul-de-sac. We moved shortly after to a large colonial on a cul-de-sac in New City, where it took me twice as long to mow the lawn and required an extra music gig each week to pay the increased mortgage.

In 2003, she wanted a new car, and I offered a brand new Honda Accord that we could pay for in cash. Instead, she insisted on a Volvo S80 for nearly twice the price. Between the colonial on a cul-de-sac and a brand new Volvo, I had locked myself in another prison that would demand more days on the road as a working musician. I was exhausted going back to school every Monday.

At one point I was given an accolade better than a Grammy. There is no higher honor for a musician than to provide the music for a fellow musician's birthday or wedding. Kenny and Kathleen Vesey, brother and sister from the band Celtic Cross, called and asked me to provide the music for their brother John's 40th Birthday party. John was the accordion player for the band. The party was scheduled for the Saturday before Memorial Day at Rory Dolan's in Yonkers. Kenny asked me to book Keith Sammut on keyboards and to set up a PA with additional microphones as there would be many musicians and singers among the attendees. As the date of the party drew near, I looked at my guitar 12 years after purchasing it, and that guitar, much like myself, still worked well, but bore the signs of its age. I went to my wife to make my case for the purchase. I had found the perfect guitar, like the one that I had seen Glenn Frey play after the Eagles reunited in 1994, for $1800. After all the work that I had done, turning over every penny to my wife, I thought it was something we could agree on. I made my case for the purchase, knowing full well that it might be rejected, and it was. I went back online and found the exact same guitar with a slight blemish selling as used for $800, and I made an executive decision and purchased it. I still remember the day I came home from school, walked in the door, and saw the large cardboard box. My wife was sitting at the kitchen table ready to dole out punishment for my defiance.

Wordlessly, I took a boxcutter, opened the box, removed the instrument from its case, and strummed that first beautiful chord. This was as close to a revolution as I had ventured thus far in my marriage. A week of stony silence followed.

Every once and a while, I would stop and take stock. I was in my early 40s and a decade of triathlons had me in peak physical condition. Every weekend, I was the guy with the guitar smiling and singing and I started to realize that women were paying attention. I became increasingly aware that women from 30 to 70 were digging what I was doing. With my marriage becoming increasingly difficult, I had a hard time turning down the offer of companionship at my gigs. Every once in a while I would get in my car to drive home from a venue and have to fight the urge to go back to the pub and see what might happen. The only thing that made me drive home was not the idea that I would be cheating on my wife, but rather that I would be cheating on my sons. The only thing keeping me in the marriage was the love I had for my two children. The marriage continued out of obligation, rather than love. I did my job as a provider and gave every bit of myself to my children. I created a life for myself caring for my boys, teaching, playing music, competing in triathlons, and surfing. I couldn't see how I could be a good father without being in the home, which is what kept me from getting divorced.

The Dark Night of the Soul

September 14, 2013 was a perfect day. It was the day of the Jersey Shore Irish Festival and I was scheduled to perform at 4 PM on the main stage with Celtic Cross. The only thing that could have made this day better was an hour of surfing. My wife took the children for a walk on the boardwalk, and I hit the waves. After an hour, I said to the one other surfer in the water "Eric, I am going to catch one more wave!" I almost made it! I was up and riding and suddenly found myself falling over the nose of my board, then made sudden impact with the ocean floor. Everything faded to black. Eric saw my body floating face down and dragged me up on the sand, starting

CPR and calling 911. I knew Eric was a high school science teacher, but what I didn't know was that he had been a lifeguard growing up on the Jersey Shore. While Eric was working on me, he was joined by a medical doctor who just happened to be walking his dog along the beach. I was defibrillated twice en route to the trauma center. I was dead and was brought back to life.

Sixteen days later, I opened my eyes in the Jersey Shore Medical Center in Neptune , NJ and tried to move. I could not get out of bed. *What the hell is going on?* I thought to myself. I tried to talk, I tried to scream, and yet I was mute. It was at that point that my sister-in-law Patty came to my bedside. She was giving my wife a break so she could return home and tend to our boys. What my sons must've been going through at this moment I have no idea, and to this day I fear to dredge up that memory. My son Kieran asked his grandfather if I was going to die, because every day the mailbox was full of cards.

Patty tried to explain what had happened. I took in only her simple words that marked the changing point in my life. "You fell off your surfboard. You hit your head on the sand. You are paralyzed, Bill."

Try to put yourself in my place. I heard that word: paralyzed. Just a moment before the accident, I had everything. I was the paratrooper, the musician, the lover, the batting practice pitcher, the swim coach, the triathlete, the surfer, the teacher. Now I had nothing, apart from the sound of the ventilator kicking into life and filling my lungs with air.

My wife and my brothers arrived at the hospital early the next day. All communication at that point was based on lip reading. In order to get anyone's attention, I made a loud farting sound with my lips. My mind was racing to all the gigs that I missed while I was in a coma. I was supposed to play Patty Bennett's father's 90th birthday the day after my accident. I was supposed to play Mary Cooney's hundredth birthday on September 21st. I was supposed to play Tommy Maloney's tailgate at West Point on September 28th.

But all of these things happened without me because I was in a medically induced coma.

I remember asking my brothers how I was supposed to eat. They told me that there was a feeding tube surgically implanted in my stomach and fluids were given through the tube. I asked how I went to the bathroom. They answered that there was a catheter in my penis, and to poop I was given an enema and rolled over on my side in the bed. The respiratory therapist came in several times a day to assess my breathing. She expressed positive thoughts and words. "Billy," she said, "you're breathing above the vent." My wife, a registered nurse, was very excited at this development; it meant that I was getting stronger. I did not know it at the time but breathing above the vent meant I was inhaling oxygen independent of the ventilator. This was a really big deal and the first positive sign after my injury. One of my doctors sat down in my room for a long talk and he said to me, "Bill, your rehab is your Olympics. This is your one chance to get back anything you possibly can. You have to go at it as hard as you possibly can." I heard his words but had difficulty processing them because there were so many other emotions competing at the same time. There was a big part of me that wanted to go back to that dark place where I was before I woke up. That 16 day coma seemed like bliss compared to the hell that I woke up to each day.

My wife pushed for me to be sent to Helen Hayes Hospital up in Stony Point, New York because it was more convenient for all of us, and she knew it would offer the best care. Helen Hayes was a short 10 minute drive from our home, and so on October 4th, a bright, beautiful, sunny day, they put my body in an ambulance and drove me the 90 miles to my new home. I was taken to the tracheotomy room, or the trach room, and introduced to my roommate. Gary Baisley was a 23-year-old man who suffered a spinal cord injury in the Hudson River one month before my accident and was a C6 quadriplegic. I was only at Helen Hayes for a few days when they detected blood in my urine. I was brought to Nyack Hospital where I was introduced to Elliott, the man who would be my urologist.

I remember feeling completely confused, as if it was all a bad dream that I would wake up from and everything would be fine. I had lost track of days and nights and I remember that all I wanted to do was to go back into that place where I was no longer awake. That was the only place that brought reprieve from my stark reality. I was helpless, but even worse, I was hopeless.

The people around me—my wife, my mom, and my brothers all tried to be upbeat in the hopes of providing some comfort for me. Sadly, all these attempts to assuage my grief were in vain. I was beyond consolation and I believe now that their attempts at being optimistic were mostly to comfort each other. All I know is that my injury was like a pebble dropped into a large pond. The ripples flowed out in every direction.

My Last Trip to the Beach

I spent a few days at Nyack Hospital getting the blood in my urine cleared up. At this time, my body was still feeling the shock of the injury and any movement could produce spasms that shook me from head to toe. The worst spasms would send my head smashing into the screws of the halo. The pain was excruciating. Without my knowing, while I was in Nyack Hospital, I experienced an eight second pause in my EKG, another myocardial infarction. More than likely it was my central nervous system going wild because of the trauma. On October 8th I returned to Helen Hayes to begin in earnest my physical, occupational, and respiratory therapy.

My physical therapist was Phil, a short, stocky man with a sense of humor that dripped with sarcasm. Phil was not the warm and fuzzy type by any stretch of the imagination. I can only imagine that this was how he coped after working for so many years on a floor that specializes in spinal cord injuries. His job every day was to move the parts of people when they were no longer able to move them on their own.

The first day that I was brought into the therapy room, I had the mobile ventilator with me blowing oxygen into my lungs. I was the only person in the room with a halo, and it became abundantly evident to me that I was the sickest guy in the room.

I think the best part of physical therapy was the FES bike. Electrode pads were attached to my lower spine and my legs, and an electric pulse produced a muscle contraction. That muscle contraction turned the pedals of the bike. For a short time every day it felt like I was back in the game, but then it was over, and I was back to complete immobility.

One of the most painful parts of physical therapy came the day when Phil put me on a bed and laid me in the prone position. It was the first time I had been prone since my accident, and the first time since I lay on top of my surfboard. The tears started to well up in my eyes, and soon they burned. Why did my tears burn? Last time I shed a tear was when my Dad was dying. Those tears did not burn; These "burning" tears must have been a result of my injury. I cried the better part of an hour and still he would not take me out of that position. I was in a blind fury. He put me in the prone position, doing what he thought he should do as a physical therapist, but to me it was an act of total insensitivity. I felt as if he were ignoring my feelings. I cried the rest of the day.

Every Saturday was shower day at Helen Hayes, and so on my first Saturday back from Nyack Hospital after the blood-in-the-urine episode, I was given a shower. The nurses undressed me, covering my naked body with towels to preserve whatever dignity I had left.

I was transferred by Hoyer lift onto a shower chair with a large tub as a basin underneath my body and was rolled down the hallway to the bathroom for my first full body shower since the injury. My nurse Kathy was an extremely pleasant person, and the perfect nurse to work the spinal cord floor. She warmed the water and started to rinse my body. When she got to my head, she started noticing debris falling into the tub underneath the shower chair. She couldn't figure out what it was, and then she did.

"Oh my God!" she exclaimed. "It's sand, Billy!" The sand that was falling out of my hair was the sand from the beach where Eric had laid my head down as he performed CPR. Amazingly, I didn't cry. To this day, I don't know why. Each grain of sand that went down the drain was a symbol of the life that I had lost. The shower was a thoroughly exhausting affair and all I wanted to do for the rest of the day was sleep. However, there would be no sleep. Just when I thought my performing days were over, I put on my bravest face and prepared for an endless stream of visitors.

It's (Not) Gonna Be Okay

My old Army buddies and friends from the Irish music world came to visit me, and I would spend the time trying to tell them that I was okay. Every single day I was barraged with questions usually along the lines of, how are you? How am I? The truth was I was desperate. I didn't have the will to live. I wished I had drowned.

I ended up having to console most of this endless stream of visitors. Ironic, isn't it?

"How are you feeling?"

"I'm going to be okay."

"How's the therapy?"

"The therapy is great. I'm getting stronger every day."

Telling people exactly what they wanted to hear became my mission. Every single day I was inundated with a barrage of visitors and well-wishers. They came from every part of my life. My friends from school would come down and spend their lunch hour with me and bring me something from the outside so I wouldn't have to eat hospital food.

All of my mother's friends from the Bronx were coming bringing cards and envelopes, all of which contained checks and cash that my wife would take home. I had no idea how much money was coming in, but I quickly deduced that it was coming in fast and furious. It was a relief to know that my wife and children would be taken care of. By this time, I had amassed enough sick time to get me through the entire academic year. My full salary and benefits would remain intact.

Somewhere along the line in those early weeks, my wife informed me that she applied for Social Security benefits for her and the children. Many of my in-laws' friends would stop by the room and again leave envelopes with checks and cash. My in-laws Tommy and Margaret moved into our house the day after my accident. They took over the duties of taking care of my children while my wife was with me in the hospital. I had always enjoyed a great relationship with my in-laws. I felt that they appreciated the life I was able to provide for their daughter.

They were both Irish born and had come to this country with nothing. My father in-law worked three jobs and had become wealthy through the sweat of his own brow.

My best friend in the whole world besides my brothers is Michael Amidenau. We became friends at the age of 14 playing freshman soccer for Albertus Magnus High School. Mike was my right fullback and I was the goalkeeper, and we had each other's backs for four years. Now, at the age of 46, we still did.

When Mike came in and sat at my bedside, I let it all out. It was the first time I heard myself say the words "I will never make love to my wife again." The tears came down in waves. I went through the litany of all the things that I would never again be able to do. I would never surf again. I would never play another note of music. I would never swim, bike, or run again in competitive triathlons. My whole life was changed forever, and the tears just kept coming.

I probably wept for the better part of an hour. Mike said that he was actually relieved. He had heard from many people how positive and upbeat I was. He said that he was worried that I was in denial. He knew then that I realized the gravity of my predicament. As I look back on it now, I really believe the person in denial was my wife. During therapy she would routinely say things like, "You will be walking in no time." I knew the truth. The doctors never tell you that you will never walk again. It's a question I never asked my rehab doctor, Dr. Fern Pomerantz. I knew the answer. There was no need to ask the question.

Tearing Off the Band-Aid

It was a Friday night when my wife told me she was going to bring the boys up to see me for the first time. My sons were 11 and 13 when my accident happened. Prior to my injury, I was ever present in their lives. I was Kieran's baseball coach, his batting practice pitcher, and his surrogate older brother. My older son Patrick is on the autistic spectrum. For Pat, I was his Social Studies and Language Arts tutor and his swim buddy. Our first house had an inground pool and I'd spend hours bouncing him up and down in the water. We first became aware that there was something different about Pat when he was two years old. At a family party, all the other kids were on the dance floor totally engaged and Pat was off to the side flapping his arms in a self-stimulating behavior. We arranged for a special education teacher to conduct an evaluation and he was enrolled in the Prime Time School. A teacher came to the house every morning for two hours and then in the early afternoon Pat boarded a bus and headed to Prime Time. He was 26 months old.

I missed my sons desperately, but as much as I wanted to see them and have them near me, I dreaded the moment when they would see me for the first time. When they finally did, they walked in the room and smiled. "Hi Dad." Once again, I put on a brave face. We had pizza together and made small talk over lunch. I'd been out of their lives for over a month, and because of that, they asked the question that broke my heart. "Daddy, when are you going to walk again?" I didn't know what to tell them.

"It's going to take a long time," I lied. All I could do was try to shield them from the horrific truth, the truth that would have to sink in over time. I can only imagine what they felt when they saw me. Kieran told me in later days that all he did for a year straight was cry every night when he got into bed. Patrick's autism, in this regard, proved to be a bit of a blessing. The autism gave him an almost natural force field from the truth. "I told you that you shouldn't have gone surfing," Pat said. "I know Pat, I know. You are absolutely right, I shouldn't have gone." After an hour, the boys left and I breathed a sigh of relief. Then I cried. I cried and cried, and then I cried some more. My sons were my whole life; I stayed in my marriage because of them. Perhaps if I had left in 2010 we would have all been better off. Maybe I would have found the happiness that I had never found with my wife. For 16 years I filled that marital bucket every single day, doing the best I could to provide a good life for her and my children. I gave up the hope of my own happiness for my children. Hindsight being 20/20, the world would have paid no mind to a divorce. I still would have been a part of my children's lives on an almost daily basis, and I know that I would have found great love because I was in the best shape of my life and had everything going for me. Of course divorce would have been a financial disaster, but that would have been better than a lifetime of pain and regret...

Every Friday the boys would come up to my room. We would have our pizza together and catch up about the week. Gradually, they got used to seeing me in the halo with the tube and the ventilator. I will never know what my injury did to my children. Everything in their world turned upside down.

CHAPTER 6

NIGHTTIME IN THE GARDEN

Every day was filled with visitors and therapy. Every night, however, was a different story altogether. The evening shift nurse, a wonderful young man named David, would come in to turn me on my side and give me an enema to help me defecate. After my bowel regime, at 10 PM, I would take my nighttime medication, which consisted of three pills. The first was Ambien, the second was Trazodone, and the last was OxyContin to dull the pain of the halo.

These medications should have been enough to give me a full night's sleep. The problem was that my despair was so intense that I could never sleep. I was desperate to try to move my body which would only trigger spasms that drove my head into the screws of the halo, unleashing a wave of horrific pain like white-hot lightning surging through my central nervous system. The speaking valve would be taken away right before bedtime so I was unable to speak. After a few hours of sleeplessness, I would make my farting noises to get the attention of the aide who was in the trach room with me and Gary all night long. She was a Haitian woman who'd come to my bedside aggravated to have been woken up from her slumber.

"What do you want?" she would ask harshly.

"I need the nurse," I would say while she tried to read my lips. "I need the nurse, I need medication to help me sleep."

My night nurse was a woman named Betty. She would come to my room again, annoyed that I was interrupting her. "You only had your medication two hours ago, you need to try to go to sleep," she would say. I would mouth the words back to her, telling her I can't sleep, I can't sleep, please give me something to knock me out. Again she would give me the same refusal. All I wanted was another OxyContin to knock me out; I could not deal with being in this state for one moment longer.

There would be no more medication for the next few hours to dull the existential pain that I felt, so what was there left for me to do but try to pray? Prior to my accident I was a, quote unquote, "good Catholic". I attended mass probably three out of four Sundays in a month, I was faithful to my wife, attentive and loving to my children, a good son, a good brother, and a good friend. When the priest would say "the Lord be with you," I would answer back "and with your spirit."

On most Sundays, I would be weary from a late night playing with the band and struggled to focus on the Scripture. I would try to give my attention to the Old Testament reading, and then to the New Testament reading, and finally the Gospel. Usually, after the first two minutes of the homily, I was gone. I would spend my time at Mass inside my own head, thinking about last night's gig and all the fun I had playing with the band and getting the crowd to their feet and out on the dance floor.

But those days in the trach room, my prayers were ones of rage at God Almighty. *How could you leave me here like this? How could you do this to me? Haven't I served you? Haven't I used gifts that you gave me for: good? Is this how you reward a faithful servant?* Some nights, my prayer would only beg for the mercy of a peaceful passing. At least my wife and children would get almost $800,000 in life insurance. It would hurt, but they could start over in good financial shape. Inasmuch as I was asking God for a merciful death, I still feared death. I feared that the Savior that I prayed to wouldn't be there. On top of my injury and all that had happened, I was now having a crisis of faith. Was my Catholic upbringing just another way to make me behave myself as a child?

When I closed my eyes and tried to pray, the images I had were of Christ in the Garden of Gethsemane during his Passion. I imagined him calling out to his father, "Please let this cup pass from me, but let your will be done." I envisioned that moment when Christ hung on the cross in Golgotha and cried out, "My God, my God, why hast thou forsaken me?" This is how I felt. This was my prayer. I was afraid to live in this state, and I was afraid to die. Not only was my body paralyzed, but now my spirit was as well.

Starting to Show the Cracks

I never paid much attention to the unusual family dynamics in my wife's family. My wife and her family members thought nothing of cutting one another out of each other's lives for extended periods of time. For the three years prior to my injury, my wife and her sister Theresa had not spoken a word to each other. There was no fight, no explanation as to why. They were friends one day, and the next, zero communication. On the day after my injury, Theresa showed up at the Trauma Hospital and apparently my wife and Theresa embraced. No explanation, no apology. Everything was wiped away.

Shortly after my injury, a Caring Bridge website was set up for well-wishers. There were several thousand messages of good tidings and prayers within a short period of time. My brothers had posted something positive about my rehabilitation progress on the website, and Meghan bristled at this. It was the first time that she and my brothers were in direct opposition. Jim was in my room with me on the day when I shrugged my shoulders for the first time. He posted this development with great delight on the Caring Bridge website. I remember clearly that it was on a Saturday when both Jim and John were with me in the room.

Soon, Meghan walked in and started screaming at them. "I told you not to put anything on the website about Bill's recovery!" She was livid and screaming and could not be calmed down. I lay in the bed watching my wife rip into my brothers for what I deemed to be nothing at all. To me there was nothing to be angry about, and yet she was. I wondered if she was angry at me for the accident and needed a scapegoat.

So I tried to rein my wife in. My brother John ushered her out into the hallway, telling her that it was not good for my recovery to see such anger. She continued screaming, and that's when John finally said it. "Meghan, you need help." My brother John had been an Army officer just like me, except he had obtained his commission at the United States Military Academy at West Point. John was now a high school history teacher at William Floyd in Mastic Beach on Long Island. He was clearly telling Meghan that she needed psychiatric help. After that confrontation, I asked my brothers not to post anything without running it by me and my wife.

Bringing up the mere idea that my wife needed therapy was almost the worst thing anyone could have said. After this incident, the battle lines between the Keenans and the Nichols were clearly drawn. This little skirmish would be the first in what would blow up to be a long protracted war, the likes of which I could never have foreseen at the moment.

My nightly agony in the garden continued through the early days of November. One night, while I was getting ready for bed, I was going through some respiratory exercises to help bring up mucus. Because I was unable to cough, there was a device called an encephalator that would assist in simulating a cough.

While going through this breathing treatment, I felt a seizure coming on. My eyes tried to express fear and I tried to speak, but with no speaking valve I couldn't communicate. After that I was gone. I woke up some 20 minutes later feeling as if I had just taken a pleasant nap. I was surrounded by doctors and nurses. My brother Jim and his wife Patty were there, as well as my wife and her father. I remember harsh words exchanged between my wife and my brother before I was placed in an ambulance and rushed to Nyack Hospital in the dead of night.

In the emergency room I became very anxious and feared that my passing could come at any minute. This was the night that I would be put to the test. The nurse came into the room where I was laying, looked at me, and said "Oh my God Billy! My name is Patsy Kivlehan. You played the music for the church service at my wedding!" I nodded and tried to whisper that I remembered her, her wedding, and her grandparents. She gave me a Xanax to calm me down. I remember whispering to her that if anything happened to me that night, my sole beneficiary would be my wife. I was admitted to the hospital and taken up to a room.

Over the next few days, I was given a battery of tests to try to find out what triggered the spasm. The eight second "pause" in my EKG was a euphemism for a heart attack. As each day and night passed, I began to believe that any moment could be my last and I tried to make peace with all that had happened. Had I been a good man, a good husband, a good father? I could never have seen it at the time, but my eight weeks of calling out to God were about to be answered.

Steven Wants to Speak With You

I spent eight days in the ICU in complete silence without my speaking valve. Somewhere around day four, a man walked into my room. "Billy, my name is Dennis Lynch," he said. "You taught my daughter Kara at Albertus. I have Steven McDonald on the phone and he wants to speak with you." A huge smile broke out on my face, my eyes opened wide. I knew very well who Steven McDonald was. He had come to speak at Albertus during my first year of teaching, and since I was the one with the PA system, I set up the microphone for him and got close to him.

Steven was an NYPD officer who was shot in 1986 by a 15-year-old-boy in Central Park. The boy shot Steven three times, the third bullet severing his spinal cord at the level of C3. From that point on, Steven would be a quadriplegic, never able to come off the ventilator. He became nationally renowned shortly after for calling the prison and forgiving his assailant. It was November 2013, 27 years after that horrible incident, and this man, a living saint, wanted to speak to me.

"Billy, God has a plan for you. It's the only reason you survived. When your rehab is over and you're stronger, you have a significant role to play. In the end, don't ever forget that there will be life, there will be life, there will be life."

Only in silence can we hear the voice of God. Because I was rushed out of Helen Hayes, there was no time for them to pack the speaking valve that would have allowed me to speak normally during the day. As it was, I lay mute for the eight days at Nyack Hospital.

When Steven called I had no choice but to be silent. If I had been able to talk I can only imagine that I would have unleashed a barrage of questions. I, or maybe he, was fortunate I did not have my speaking valve. As I sit here writing in 2020, I swear that my inability to speak was by God's design. My silence allowed God's message to come not *from* Steven but *through* Steven. My cries out to God on a nightly basis were answered by that phone call. I could not possibly have known it at the time, but I was being called. It is a calling that I've answered in the affirmative even if at times I have rebelled against it. I am being called to suffer so that others can see how to cope with their own suffering. I can only pray that I am worthy of the calling.

I could never have known what that one ten minute phone call would begin. I could never have known that Steven's call would be my catalyst back to a life that would impact thousands of people. I say this not as a "look at how great I am," but rather as a statement of fact.

Another few days passed and the doctors decided to put in a pacemaker because they had not determined the cause of the seizure. They performed the surgery and some days later I was back at Helen Hayes to continue my rehab. That ten minute talk with Steven was still running through my mind when my Principal, a fellow Albertus and Fordham alum, Dr. Michael Gill, came by my room for a visit. Mike stayed for about 20 minutes and just as he was about to leave I told him, "Mike, I am coming back to work!" I don't know what made me say it, or what made me think that it was even possible, but Steven's words lingered with me; maybe I did have a role to play. The only thing that I thought I might be able to do was teach. Despite my several minutes underwater, I had not suffered a traumatic brain injury. All of my cognitive abilities remained intact. My memory was as sharp as always. As I began my afternoon therapy, I excitedly told my speech therapist about my plan to return to teaching.

"Billy, that's fantastic!" she responded. There's only one little problem...you still can't breathe."

Jaclyn and the First Great Hurdle

Jaclyn, my speech therapist, was the most important woman in my life. Jaclyn was the person who presented the first great hurdle during my stay at Helen Hayes. I had to show Jaclyn that I would be able to swallow, so one of the first mornings that we met, she conducted a bronchoscopy. The scope revealed that I would indeed be able to swallow and so, of course, I proceeded to order a cheeseburger, fries, and a Coke. Prior to this moment, my only nutritional intake had been through the feeding tube.

I liked Jaclyn Offito immediately. She was yet another in a line of interesting and funny women taking care of me. Above all, she was compassionate. I had wonderful therapists during my time at Helen Hayes, but some of them lacked the compassion that I perceived in Jaclyn.

Jaclyn informed me that my paralysis was so high that the medical staff did not predict that I'd be able to ever breathe independently again, which would leave me tethered to a ventilator for the remainder of my days. Without independent breathing I would never be able to return to teaching.

So, in that moment of crisis, I developed the following thought process: If I can learn to breathe, I can talk. If I can talk, I can teach.

If I can teach, my life will have meaning again. My life will have a purpose. I will have a reason to go on living. I will show my sons that this is how a man stands up in the middle of withering adversity. I will show my wife that even in this wretched condition I can still be a good provider for my family. I will show my wife that I am not someone to be discarded.

---------------- CHAPTER 7 ----------------

JUST BREATHE!

O nce Jaclyn saw how serious I was about my goal, she set out to help me in every way she could. What this meant was closing the door to my room and taking me off the ventilator, something that Jaclyn had been told never to do.

We started by taking me off the vent for one minute. As I struggled to breathe, my eyes got wide with fear. I felt like a fish flopping around on the deck of a charter boat. After I would regain my breath, I was then introduced to a God-awful pipe called the breather, a device used for people just like me to help them get back some lung function. The breather features resistance on both the inhalation and exhalation: this was my Olympics. The more I used the breather, the stronger I got. The stronger I got, the longer I was able to remain off the ventilator.

As Christmas approached, our work moved into a more practical arena. Jaclyn brought in a bag of green and red balloons, and I began to fill up the balloons one at a time, writing a letter on each balloon to spell out Merry Christmas. Each balloon took me longer than five minutes to fill up one breath at a time. This continued for many days.

By Christmas I could function off the ventilator for 20 to 30 minutes at a time. It was then that Jaclyn had the incredible idea to go down to the first floor auditorium and sit 15 rows back.

"Now Billy," she called to me on our first day there. "I want you to teach me history lessons." So I started to teach her lessons about Napoleon Bonaparte, Winston Churchill, and the causes of World War I. Jaclyn would sit in the old auditorium and when my volume got low, she would yell. " Louder Billy! I can't hear you!" She drove me relentlessly with a smile on her face and love in her heart. With each passing day, I became more and more convinced that I could actually return to teaching.

This is not to say that there were not very difficult times during my therapy sessions with Jaclyn. The more time we spent together, the more I began to open up to her about all of the things that I was feeling. These were things that I did not feel I could share even with my wife, including my lost manhood. I shared my fears about potentially losing my life and all of my grief for the man that I had lost.

Several times we started to work and I just cried. Jaclyn would shut the door, turn out the lights, and just listen. She would wipe the tears from my eyes when they just kept coming, seemingly without end. When I was done crying, we got right back to work.

There was one exercise in particular I remember which brought on a fit of tears like no other: singing karaoke. I asked for some of the big songs that I used to sing with the band, and I started out okay. But once the notes got a little bit high my voice cracked, faltered, and then it was game over, another round of tears. And just like that I begged her to turn it off and to relieve me of the painful reminder of what I had lost.

Making It Work

Relations between the Keenans and the Nichols had considerably deteriorated by this point. My wife was still coming to the hospital as soon as the boys were off to school. Around 3 PM, she would leave the hospital to go home and help them with their homework before leaving them with my in-laws and returning to the hospital for dinner. As I look back on it now after all that has transpired,

I believe that she was trying very hard to do the right thing. At least she appeared as if she were trying to do the right thing.

I believe that despite all of her medical training as a registered nurse, she was in denial of my actual condition. It appeared she could not come to grips with the fact that I would never be the same man again. This was the same intransigence and refusal to believe that she could ever be wrong that I'd seen in my marriage for 16 years prior to my injury. I had asked her to attend marriage counseling in 2010 and ended up going to see the counselor four times by myself. During that summer I spent two months sleeping alone in the guest room. I never asked myself, "What's my next move if she never comes to counseling?"

As Thanksgiving came closer, I was informed that my sister-in-law Theresa and her husband would be bringing the Thanksgiving dinner to Helen Hayes and we would be reserving the quiet room on the spinal cord injury floor to have the feast.

The mere fact that Theresa was now playing such a huge role in our lives had me confused. This was the woman who punched my wife in the eye so hard while we were dating that Meghan missed a week of work. This was the woman who had cut off all contact with my wife three years prior to my injury. Now, she was making the Thanksgiving dinner.

On the afternoon of the holiday I was wheeled into the quiet room and dinner began. Everyone seemed in a very happy mood, and the food was delicious. I even told Theresa that I was glad she had come back into our lives. These words would come back to bite me in the ass in the worst way.

After dinner ended my boys gave me a kiss goodbye and were picked up by someone in my family and taken to my brother Jim's house in Stony Point where the Keenans were getting together.

After Thanksgiving dinner when everyone left and I was back in my room, the thought occurred to me that the conversations that needed to take place between me and my wife never happened. We were never able to look each other in the eye and say what really needed to be said. This was a common theme throughout our marriage. The only thing that kept us together was our kids. Even after making love I had never been able to look her in the eye and see anything beyond the surface. After that horrible summer of 2010, it was all about making it work. And now my spinal cord injury was all about making it work. My injury, just like my marriage, was something that needed to be managed..

Keenan Strong

The Irish community in New York is famous for coming together to put on benefit fundraising concerts when a member of that community falls ill or is subject to a traumatic injury such as mine. When the Keenan Strong committee was formed, I requested my friend Martin, a highly successful entrepreneur, to head it up. Naturally, all of New York's best Irish bands had volunteered to perform. I was told later on that at the first meeting there was a good deal of crying as people were still trying to come to grips with what had happened.

My understanding is that in very short order, my sister-in-law Theresa worked her way into the day-to-day leadership and running of the committee. The dates May 3rd and May 4th of 2014 would be the dates of Keenan Strong weekend. The weekend-long festival was to be the mother of all Irish-American benefit concerts, set to take place in three separate locations.

I was largely kept out of the loop of any of the goings on by the committee. It did become evident early on that there was a good bit of tension between the Nichols family and certain members of my own family. I would only come to know of the extent of the problems after the fact.

Christmas came and went and I was still at Helen Hayes. Jaclyn and I continued to work towards the goal of breathing without the ventilator. After working with Jaclyn for several months I was able to stay off the vent for five hours at a time.

In the middle of January, a miracle happened. I don't remember what day of the week it was. All I remember was Dr. Pomerantz coming into my room and very quickly giving a sharp pull in my throat and the tracheostomy was gone. From that moment on, I was breathing on my own. This was the happiest moment I had since my injury; it might've been the only happy moment that I had since my injury. I was getting very good at putting on a brave face for my visitors and for my children, but deep inside I had a sadness that I had only expressed to the respiratory therapist Russ. Russ would administer nebulizer treatments four times per day, always making sure to ask me if there was anything I needed before he left the room. "Russ," I told him one day, "there is no pill to cure a broken heart."

The next major hurdle in my recovery was to get rid of the dreaded halo. A series of x-rays were done to assess the healing in my neck before it was determined that the Halo could be removed. I vividly remember the day. A few of my teacher friends from North Rockland were there to visit me, and quite a few of the nursing staff and caregivers gathered in my room to actually witness the event. Apparently, it was a sight that very few of them had seen before.

A neurologist from outside the hospital was called in to perform the removal of the halo. I was not prepared for the pain that accompanied this procedure. My skin had started to grow around the screws that attached the device to my skull, so with the removal of each screw my skin was torn away, causing excruciating pain.

When it was finally done, the neurologist put on a hard, white, plastic cervical collar, called a Philadelphia collar. Everyone in the room was clapping and cheering and high-fiving. I did my best to smile and join in the party, but I was still more focused on all that I had lost. My time at Helen Hayes was now drawing to a close and there were plans being made to send me to a subacute facility to get me stronger before I could return home. At this point in my post injury life, I had become completely dependent on Meghan. She, more than anyone else, was my lifeline. What I did not fully grasp at the time, was that there were several options on the table when my time at Helen Hayes ran out.

Five months post injury, I was breathing independently and feeling stronger with each passing day. There was absolutely no reason why I could not have been brought home at this point. I had been away from my boys for five months and had desperately wanted to return home. In order to bring me home, our house needed to be renovated to make it handicapped accessible. I would need a ramp to get me from the driveway onto the deck and in through the sliding glass doors to the kitchen. In addition, a new bathroom would need to be built. This bathroom would need to be large enough to accommodate two caregivers and a shower chair. Finally, I would need a hospital bed and an electric Hoyer lift to transfer me from the wheelchair to the bed.

There was more than enough money to execute these renovations. Four Keenan relatives wrote $10,000 checks immediately after my injury. My cousin Marian Adams was able to secure a $10,000 donation from the Andy K foundation. The North Rockland teachers held a fundraiser one week before Thanksgiving and raised an additional $30,000. Unsolicited donations were flowing in on a daily basis. My old friend Janet Cooney dropped off a check for $5,000. The guys from Saint Joseph Gaelic Football Club dropped off another check for the same amount. Besides this, my regular salary was going straight into my HSBC account and Social Security had already kicked in. Much of the money brought in during this time was cash; it is impossible to know the exact amount. However, based on bank statements and eyewitness accounts, it is safe to say that the approximate amount was near $200,000. When the insurance company MVP notified Helen Hayes that February 20th was to be my final day for which they would continue to pay, there was plenty of money to modify the house and bring me straight home. This is what should have happened.

The second option was for me to remain at Helen Hayes on the first floor which was for subacute care. I would receive one hour of physical therapy each day and full time nursing care. Meghan argued against this option, because in her opinion I needed more than just one hour of physical therapy. It was almost as if she was still under the impression that somehow I was going to walk again. If I had been able to remain at Helen Hayes, I would have been able to play an active role in the production of my CD that I had started to record in April of 2012. I would have been able to spend time at North Rockland high school as a guest teacher to prepare for my return.

There were wonderful facilities in Bergen County, NJ where I could have continued my rehabilitation, but my wife had fallen under the sway of a woman named Maria Martino whose husband was also a patient at Helen Hayes. Tony Martino was a man in his early 60s who had become quadriplegic at his grandson's third birthday while playing in a bounce house. Maria and Tony lived in Monticello, New York, where there was a nursing home near them called Achieve that apparently had very good physical, occupational, and speech therapy. My wife and her father went with Maria to view the facilities. Without going to see any other facilities, the decision was made by Meghan and her father. On February 20th I would be sent to Achieve in Liberty, New York - 70 miles away from my friends and my family.

CHAPTER 8

POSTCARDS FROM THE CHÂTEAU

It was with a sense of dread that I prepared to leave Helen Hayes. I was angry. I did not know why I was being sent 70 miles away. My wife insisted that the therapy was excellent, but how could she not realize that no amount of therapy was going to have me up and walking?

My roommate Gary had been taken home immediately after his stay at Helen Hayes. Before Gary left, a large benefit was held for him in a local banquet hall. The money raised was enough to modify his parents house to make it accessible for him to get in and out. I wasn't sure how much money had been coming in for me, but I knew it was a large amount.

All the nursing staff were gathered outside in the hallway to bid me farewell. I kept my head down, started to wheel away, and over the back of my shoulders called goodbye. It was just too difficult to leave. I was facing the unknown. All I did know was that I was being ripped out of a place where I had found safety for five months. I was going into a deep dark unknown. I was loaded onto an Ambulette with one driver. It was just me and the driver, no wife and no caregiver. Just me and a stranger.

The trip out of Helen Hayes onto the Palisades Parkway was relatively painless. By the time we hit Route 17, however, every bump caused my body to go into spasm. The spasticity was so intense that within a few miles, my body was completely twisted out of position in the chair. The driver took pity on my condition and stopped the van on the shoulder and tried to rearrange my parts. Once again after about 10 more miles, the spasms had kicked in again and I was a tight and twisted wreck. After one more attempt to straighten out my body, the driver gave up, put his head down, and continued the trip.

It was late in the afternoon and the sun was almost down when I pulled into the driveway of Achieve Nursing Home in Liberty, New York. As I rolled into the lobby, my heart sank. This was a miserable place. This was not Helen Hayes. What the hell was I doing here?

One of the nurses met me in the lobby and brought me to the elevator. My wife was already upstairs with Maria in Tony's room which was two doors away from mine and everyone seemed to be in great spirits. Tony was surrounded by a bunch of his friends from Monticello. Everyone greeted me warmly, but there was one problem. They were all complete strangers in their 50s and 60s. I was 46 years old, still struggling to let go of the triathlete, the surfer, the musician, the teacher, the father, the husband. Why was I here?

Shortly after I got to my room I was introduced to my physical therapist, my occupational therapist, and my speech therapist. They used the Hoyer lift to get me from the wheelchair onto the bed, and started to make initial assessments with a brief range of motion exercise with both my legs, arms, and hands.

I was told that the second floor was a rehab floor, and that everyone there was working towards going home. My wife stayed for about an hour and then said that she had to get home and help the boys with their homework.

The nurses came in around 9 PM to do my nighttime bowel regimen. As I lay on my side waiting for the big event, I started to feel panic. I felt alone in a foreign place deserted by family and friends. Once again the nagging questions came. Why the hell was I here? Wasn't there an alternative closer to home? Anxiety overtook me and the Ambien and Trazodone could not get me to sleep. I spent the night watching SportsCenter on ESPN. Of course, it repeats every hour. Is this hell? It damn sure feels like it.

As I said before, the second floor was supposed to be a rehab floor. The first and third floors were for long-term nursing care. Old people came to die in Achieve. It was their final destination. Achieve was owned and operated by Orthodox Jews, which meant there would be no daily Eucharist like there was at Helen Hayes. There would be no 5 PM Saturday evening mass with Father Jim McKenna from the Marian Shrine.

When the first and third floors were full and a bed was needed for nursing home patients, the patient would be placed on the second floor. During that first hellish night, I was kept awake by the screams of dementia patients. I screamed out, "Why don't you just die?"

I was in the room with the baby monitor and the other baby monitor was at the nurses' station out in the hallway. When I needed help or to change the channel or a drink or a cookie I called into the baby monitor. The nurses aides were continually busy on the night shift. Very often my calls for help went unanswered for up to an hour. When I finally fell asleep, they came in every two hours to turn me so I didn't get a pressure ulcer.

When my wife arrived the next day, I asked her when I could come home. I needed to get the hell out of there immediately. She answered "I'm not taking you home unless you get off the junk. You need to get off the sleep medication or I am not taking you home!" Her answer left me completely baffled. Didn't she want me to come home? Exhausted and confused, I barely made it to therapy that day. When the night nurse came in to administer the Ambien and Trazodone, I declined my night meds. If getting off sleep medication was what it would take for me to come home, I was going to get to work immediately. A second sleepless night ensued. I knew lack of sleep would hinder my ability to participate fully in my rehabilitation sessions, but I was determined to refuse the sleep meds.

By the time they came to get me the next morning for therapy, I looked like hell. My therapist asked me what had happened, to

which I answered, "I declined my sleep medication last night."
"Why would you do such a thing?" I told him what my wife said
to me the night before. He was shocked. When my wife arrived a
little bit later that morning, they pulled me out of therapy and into
a meeting room. The director of nursing was there along with my
wife and several other staff members. Again, they wanted to know
why I rejected my night meds. I explained. I wanted to go home. I
did not want to be there.

I told them what my wife had said, that the only way that I would
be allowed to go home was if I got off the narcotics. The nursing staff
looked to my wife demanding an explanation. She was a registered
nurse and knew better. She was being called on the carpet by other
professionals, and there was no place for her to hide. As I recall, she
said nothing. The director of nursing stressed how very important
it was for me to get a good night's sleep, so I could get the most out
of therapy. The meeting concluded with everyone agreeing that I
would go back on the sleep medication.

I remember very well the day that my sons Pat and Kieran came
up for their first visit at Achieve. My friend Kathleen from the band
Celtic Cross and her Mom were also there. My wife, my two sons,
my sister-in-law Theresa, and her husband, and his two children
were all there at this time. The boys stayed for about an hour and I
tried to engage them in conversation. We were in the lobby of the
second floor, and there was nothing to keep them occupied. The
visit was quite short and they left with Theresa and her husband for
The Castle on Route 17, one of those places where you can drive go
carts and have all sorts of fun. I told my nurse the next morning that
I did not want my children to come up to Achieve again. "Why?" she
asked. "This is a depressing place," was my response.

My wife arrived the next day as I was beginning my therapy.
She made a beeline for the therapy room and asked me, "What did
you say to the nursing staff?" I told her that I had simply said that I
didn't want the boys here because achieve was a depressing place.
She told me that I should not say such things. I couldn't imagine

why anybody would give two shits about my thoughts on Achieve. They were being paid with the insurance money, so why shouldn't I say what I thought?

As I look back on it, I'm left with so many questions. Why was I not given a laptop and Dragon software so that I could communicate with the outside world? Why was Achieve the only place that my wife considered? My cousin Patricia worked part-time at a place in Woodcliff Lake. Why was I not taken there, so that I could see my friends and my family? The answer to these questions is really quite troubling. Only later did I realize I was placed in Achieve on purpose. There were forces at work that wanted me away from the family unit.

In early March, my Godmother Aunt Lizzie Brady and her husband Dan made the trek from Blauvelt, New York up to Achieve. They stayed for about an hour, and on their way home, my Aunt Liz called back to the room and asked "Billy, why don't you have a van?" She expressed the thought that I should be able to come home on weekends, and then voiced a thought far too generous: she offered to buy me a van.

"No, no, Aunt Liz! There's plenty of money that was donated, Meghan just hasn't spent the money." Another question: why had she not purchased an accessible vehicle?

On the day of the Pearl River Irish parade, my cousin Joe O'Brien brought me home. Joe shared a two family house with his wife's brother who was wheelchair-bound and they owned an accessible van. Joe and my wife made the trip up to Liberty to collect me and I was brought home and given a steak dinner. Then it was off to Felix Festa Middle School for my son Patrick's drama production. Being home after six months felt almost surreal. I wanted to stay. I wanted everything to be the way it was before I got hurt. I didn't want to leave my sons.

When I told my wife that my Aunt Liz had offered to buy a vehicle, I think she was actually shamed into looking for one. And so the "Popemobile" was purchased at the end of March. Honestly it was, and still is, a pretty horrible looking vehicle. I call it the "Popemobile" because it is the color white and the body type is a cross between a London taxi cab and a big bubble. The one good thing about it was that it was built from the ground up to be handicapped accessible. Once the vehicle was purchased, Meghan was able to bring me home during the day on the weekends.

In early March, a large benefit was held in Lantana, Florida at the Shamrock Club. We received a call the next day informing us that $60,000 had been raised. We were amazed! Why was I not brought home then? What was I still doing up at Achieve? My friend Shaun McHugh had built the ramps to get me from the driveway into the back sliding deck door. All I needed was a handicapped accessible bathroom.

Many months later, Shaun told me that after he finished building the ramps he came into the house to talk to my father-in-law. "Tommy, I finished building the ramps and now I want to know when we can get started building a bathroom for Billy. I've got all the guys, all I need are the materials." My father-in-law turned to Shaun. "No hurry building the bathroom. Billy is never coming home from that nursing home; a common cold could kill him; he is that weak." Meanwhile, I was getting stronger by the day.

The reason I call this chapter Postcards from the Château d'If is because of an experience I had in my early days of teaching at North Rockland High School. I was looking for reading material, and I took a walk to the school library and started rummaging through the fiction section. It was then that I saw a collection of the works of Alexander Dumas. The first book I selected was *The Three Musketeers*. After that I picked up *The Man in the Iron Mask*. And then it was on to the book that would become my favorite work of fiction, *The Count of Monte Cristo*.

This is the story of the sailor Edmund Dantes. He was wrongfully accused and convicted of treason and sent to the island prison Château d'If. In the film adaptation, the evil warden tells Edmund, "I know you are innocent." Edmund endured 14 years in that prison. As I look back on it now, I begin to realize that I was Edmund Dantes, sent 70 miles away from my family and friends through no fault of my own. Was I no longer of any use to my wife?

I was isolated. Who could possibly make the time to take the trek up Route 17 to Liberty, New York? Everyone was busy with their jobs and families. I knew people would like to make the trip, but it was just too difficult. And so I endured my isolation. The crime for which I was being accused, tried, convicted, and imprisoned was the simple act of surfing. During the eight years of my surfing life, my wife went to extraordinary lengths to find ways to keep me from the ocean. Even when I made it to the ocean I was made to feel guilty for going. This only made me covet this precious time all the more. My wife and her family could never understand the simple concept of joy. They were, as time revealed, a group of people who were so incapable of experiencing joy that they could not understand it when they saw it in me. For every day that I enjoyed in the ocean, several days of guilt on my part or silence on hers followed.

My time at Achieve marched on and I fell into the routine of therapy during the day, with my wife being there for nearly all of it. At 4 PM she left to go home and help the boys with their homework. Maria Martino very often brought me dinner, and day after day they invited me to Tony's room afterwards. I went down to visit a few times, but after a while, I preferred to be alone.

I was basically alone from 4 PM until 7 AM the next morning. Of course, the nursing staff did come in periodically to conduct vital signs checks and to administer medications. The highlight of the night was getting transferred from the wheelchair to my bed. I started doing this earlier and earlier.

What I needed was a laptop. I had been trained in the use of Dragon software by the technology therapist at Helen Hayes and would have been able to connect with friends on Facebook or email if it had been made available to me. A laptop was purchased for me by Meghan's brother, but it was not given to me. Instead that very same laptop was brought up to Achieve only to get me to dictate an email to the Keenan Strong committee. The email was to be directed to members of my own family asking them to cooperate with my wife's sister Theresa. She had seized control of the committee that was working to raise funds for my 24-hour care. I had expressly appointed my friend Martin to head the committee, as it was my wish that no blood relative be in direct charge of it. Seventy miles away, my wishes were ignored.

Martin was greatly impressed by Theresa's business acumen and organizational abilities. He largely stepped back from the day-to-day workings of the committee. My brother Jim bristled at the idea that Theresa was taking such an active role in heading the committee. The police officer in Jim believed something was amiss, but when he complained he was shot down and quickly marginalized by Theresa. My Keenan cousins suppressed their instinct to object to Theresa and her methods, and set their energy to the task of making the fundraiser as successful as it could be.

The nurses aides on the floor would come in every two hours to reposition me so as to prevent any skin breakdown from pressure ulcers. These hours, alone in my room, were the first times that I ever experienced true loneliness. I spent my whole life in the middle of the party. The joy that I expressed in my music and found in my classroom drew so many wonderful people into my life. I loved teaching. I grew more and more relaxed in the classroom and began to show my true personality. I kept a guitar in the class and every once in a while out of nowhere I would just pick it up and play a song for the students. I was born to be around people, to be the life of the party, and it devastated me to know I would never be able to play "Banana Pancakes" for my senior psychology class again. My world, which at one time knew only the limits of my imagination, was reduced to a wheelchair, a bed, and a hospital room. Loneliness, more than any other aspect of my condition, truly made me feel, *crippled*.

It's important to note that at this time I still had no reason to suspect any wrongdoing. Meghan was coming every day and I thought that we were going to be okay. I appreciated all my in-laws were doing by giving up everything and moving into my house to take care of the boys. Naturally, I was upset at the tension between our two families, but 70 miles away, I was removed from the goings-on of the Keenan Strong Committee.

There were difficult days during my time in Liberty. On one particular day, I woke covered in my own excrement. My caregiver Trina cleaned me up, got me ready for the day, put me in the wheelchair, and sent me down to the therapy room. Very shortly after I arrived, I did it again. One of the therapists smelled it and sent me back up to the room. This was a complete loss of dignity. How could this be? This is not who I was! I was a five foot nine, 180 pound infant. The tears flowed and I wept in silence. Trina did not know how to respond. She sent me back down to the therapy room and as I was wheeled back to the therapy space, I had a full-blown meltdown.

Andrew, the physical therapy assistant, was quick to detect my state of mind. He and Sylvia Brennan brought me to a private area, and I just fell apart. Now I wasn't weeping in silence, I was weeping out loud. I guess it was bound to happen. My heart was broken in a million pieces by the injury and now I cried out of loneliness, desolation, and complete loss of dignity. I was faced with the most difficult questions. How do I find a way forward? What is the point of living like this? I retreated to the silence of my room and resolved that the next day would be better. Thankfully, Meghan was not there then to see me in that state.

Time marched on after that day.

CHAPTER 9

KEENAN STRONG

The Keenan Strong fundraiser was a multi-layered effort to raise as much money as possible. The concerts were going to be the major part of the fundraiser. There were three concerts scheduled. On Saturday May 3rd there would be a concert at the Irish American Center in Mineola Long Island and at the same time another one at Rory Dolan's in Yonkers. On Sunday May 4th, the largest of the events was to be held at the German Masonic fairgrounds in Tappan. $100 raffle tickets were for sale, and those were sold to a variety of people throughout the tri-state area. Every ticket stub and dollar went straight to Theresa. The first flier that was produced by the committee stated the goal of the fundraiser "to raise as much money as possible for the 24 hour care of Billy Keenan." Theresa quickly changed the stated goal of Keenan Strong "to raise as much money as possible for the Keenan family."

One year before my accident, I had started to record a CD. George Rigney, Derek Sherry, and I met up in Gary Solomon's studio in Stony Point. We started laying down the basic tracks for nine songs. The sessions were held over my Easter break from school. Naturally, I made most of the mistakes that musicians make in recording a CD. You should be very well rehearsed and know exactly what you're doing so as not to waste precious studio time. The bills rack up very quickly. We recorded a few songs: "The Craic

Was 90," "My Hometown on the Foil," "The Homes of Donegal," "Nancy Spain," "The Banks of the Roses," and more.

The songs were standard and, of course, as I look back on it now, I wish that I had pushed the boundaries and recorded exactly what I wanted to sing, not what my audience wanted to hear. If given a Mulligan, I would've recorded some of the same songs but with different tempos—much slower, much more contemplative. I did as much as I could over that Easter break and then time got away from me. My performance schedule became jam packed and the project lay dormant and unfinished.

When I got hurt, my friends from the Irish music world went to Gary's studio and finished my album. They added flutes, fiddles, accordions, mandolins, banjos, and backing vocals. My friend Pat, the bass player from Celtic Cross, stepped in to co-produce and organize all the musicians who volunteered to help. Gary and Pat did an amazing job and my fellow musicians put their hearts and souls into the project and made something truly beautiful. I will be forever grateful for what they did with my music!

Two thousand copies of the CD were printed and ready for sale online, as well as at the Keenan Strong festival events.

My wife drove the Popemobile, my white wheelchair-accessible van which looked like an enlarged London taxi cab, up to Liberty and picked me up for the May 4th event. I was dressed in a pair of khakis with a blue button down shirt. The cervical collar was around my neck and instead of contacts I wore glasses, as I had since my accident. As we drove down I listened once again to my finished CD. The speakers in my vehicle were quite crappy, but I was still thrilled to hear my voice coming through them. I was excited to see all my old friends again, but I was also nervous. This would be the first time that many people would see me in this condition. How would they react? Would they cry? Would they make awkward conversation and say things like "You look great!" I knew I didn't look great. I looked like I had been hit by a truck.

By the time we arrived at the German Masonic ground in Orangeburg, a large crowd was present. The first event on the docket for the day was a Catholic Mass said by my dear friend Father Rob McKeon. Mass was held under a large tent. My wife and children and I were up at the front on the right side of the altar.

As soon as Mass concluded, I rolled out a few feet before I was inundated with people stopping to talk to me. I was so happy just to be around people once again! It felt very much like being at my own wake, but I was alive to see it. Most notably, my former girlfriend Sara, whispered into my ear that the song "Pretty Little Girl from Omagh" from my CD, warmed her heart. When I tried to win her back in 1995, I took her to the Tara on Midland Ave. in Yonkers. Andy Cooney's band got me up to sing, and I played that song. It had been 19 years since that night and she still remembered that song. I think it was her way of telling me that her feelings for me never changed. I know, for my part, that every day when I passed by her street on my way to work, I thought of her.

After greeting as many people as I possibly could, I excused myself by saying that I wanted to go hear a little bit of music. My own band, The Prime Time Show Band, was on stage doing their thing, and my spot had been taken by Peter McKiernan. It felt surreal and it was a little bit of a gut punch to see my band on stage minus their leader.

Celtic Cross took the stage next and they were in great form. I had filled in many nights for their guitar player Walter and their bassist Pat Dineen. I knew their repertoire as well as any band member. Kenny, Kathleen, and John Vesey were the heart and soul of Celtic Cross. I know that they were personally devastated by my accident, but they were on stage doing their best to make the benefit a huge success.

As I looked around at a sea of people I estimated there had to be about 6,000 people at the event. "I will never have to worry about money again!" I thought to myself. In the middle of Celtic Cross's set, I was called up near the stage to be honored by the County executive Ed Day, who read a proclamation declaring May 4th to be Billy Keenan Day in Rockland County.

After he had finished, I asked for the microphone to be held close so that I could say a few words. A cheer rang out from the crowd. I leaned forward and spoke into the microphone.

"For those of you who can hear my voice, I want you to know that this is not the end of me. I am going to find a way back. I am going to find a way to contribute. This is just the beginning!" These were not prepared remarks. They came from my heart and my soul. Without being fully cognizant of it, I was echoing the words that Steven had spoken to me that bleak day in November when I lay helpless and mute in Nyack Hospital. I doubt that there was a soul there who knew the goal that I'd set for myself. I was coming back to teach. There was not a doubt in my mind. No matter what it took, I was going to make this happen.

Shortly after I made my remarks, a rain shower came. Everyone went running and I was quickly ushered back up the ramp into the van. The shower stopped quickly, and I came back down the ramp only to be engulfed by another round of visitors and well-wishers. Out of nowhere the familiar sight of a man named Greg Kelly, the host of Good Morning New York on Fox Five, approached. I couldn't believe that it was him.

"How the hell did you end up here?" I asked him. He laughed. "I heard your interview with Sean Adams on WCBS AM, and I knew I had to be here!" I was absolutely overjoyed.

I wanted to get back closer to hear the music, but I was swamped by people, and it continued like that for much of the rest of the day. The Cable Beverage company donated 80 kegs of beer, so the booze was all profit. My CD, Keenan Strong t-shirts, and Keenan Strong wristbands were for sale; raffle tickets were going like hotcakes. My Keenan cousins organized a raffle which generated over $35,000. Every penny was turned over to my sister-in-law Theresa. Everyone trusted that the right thing would be done with the money.

The one band I wanted to see most was The Cunningham Brothers. I thought for sure they'd be at the Rockland event, but my wife had arranged for them to play at the event in Mineola the night before. In a day filled with happiness, this was the one bit of sadness and disappointment. As I look back at it now, I wonder if it was Meghan's final blow in a grudge against The Cunningham Brothers that had lasted two decades. I believe that she never forgave Jim Cunningham for booking my band to play a wedding on the day that she wanted to be married. I believe that she never forgave me for insisting that the Cunninghams play at our wedding. I had been dealing with her grudge throughout my marriage.

The Counting Room

This is the part of the story where I have to step back and rely on the words of someone who was there. I was out on the fairgrounds near the stage playing my part as "poster child" for the Keenan strong fundraiser. I don't know what happened inside the kitchen of the fairgrounds, otherwise known as "the counting room." I needed the help of a true investigator. That person is my uncle Kevin Keenan, a retired NYPD detective. What follows is a summary of the things Kevin witnessed on May 4.

According to Kevin, "There were several money collecting stations at the fairground. Throughout the day, Marion Keenan Adams (my cousin) and Tommy Nichols (my father-in-law) would go together, collect the money, and bring it to the counting room." In the words of Kevin Keenan, "the Nichols family completely controlled the counting room. They only allowed one Keenan family member at a time to be present in the counting room. There were many other non-Keenan people in the counting room." Uncle Kevin told me that my brothers were outside doing the grunt work. I would come to find out later that my sister-in-law Theresa had sent a text to another committee member saying, "Keep Jimmy and John Keenan away from the money! I do not trust them!" They were marginalized and given the role of foot soldiers for the day, organizing volunteers, emptying garbage, parking cars–all the dirty work that the Nichols did not want to do."

Uncle Kevin continued, "Each member of the counting team was told to break down the money into denominations of $100 bills, $50 bills, $20 bills, $10 bills, $5 dollar bills, and $1 bills. The checks were also to be separated. Rather than count up a dollar value, the counters were told to only count the number of the denominations. By doing it this way, none of the counters were able to report an exact dollar amount. The money was placed in large yellow envelopes with only the denominations, and the number of each denomination written on the outside of the envelope. Each envelope was placed in the freezer."

"I was in the counting room at 10 PM when all of the money had been broken down into denominations and placed into envelopes in the freezer. I watched as 18 envelopes were placed in a cooler. The cooler (ice chest) was given to Rob Smith, a retired NYPD police detective and the next-door neighbor of the Nichols family." He had the responsibility of guarding the money until the next day.

Another fundraiser had taken place the night before. I had a great number of supporters that I had won over the years of playing at the Irish-American Center on Willis Ave., in Mineola Long Island. On May 3rd, the Keenan Strong Festival in Mineola took place. The woman in charge of that branch of the committee was Liz McKenna, a close friend of the Nichols family. I had known Liz for quite a while and had no reason to distrust her. During the final week of the meetings leading up to the Long Island event, the committee decided that the proceeds from the evening would be given over to John Callahan. John was retired from the NYPD and a close friend of the Keenan family. John would drive with the proceeds and deliver them to the Keenan household in Stony Point. This was the residence of my brother Jim, also a retired NYPD officer. At the final meeting before the concert, a change in plan was announced. Liz McKenna announced that the proceeds were to be held in the safe at the Mineola Center until a Nichols family member could come and collect them.

Between the money in Mineola and the cooler guarded by Rob Smith, all of the proceeds from the fundraiser would be under the control of the Nichols family. The only money that was ever under control of the Keenan's was the $35,000 raised from the raffle... which they also turned over to Theresa.

I left to go back to the nursing home around 8:30 PM. I was so happy with the turnout and buzzing from all the activity. Over the course of the day, a great many people had come up to me with beer, and I was so excited that I drank a little bit too much. By the time I got back to Achieve in Liberty and got ready for bed, I sat up and vomited. My wife slept at the home of the Martinos that night, while my in-laws slept in a hotel room with my sons. Later I found out why my in-laws slept in a hotel that night. They were afraid our home could be invaded by thieves looking to steal the funds that were raised.

A great many of my therapists from Achieve came down for the benefit. The morning after, I was tired and a bit hungover, but very happy to begin therapy knowing that so many people still cared.

Behind Enemy Lines

On May 11, 2014, exactly one week after the final Keenan Strong event, I returned home for a Mother's Day barbecue. None of the Keenans were there, only my in-laws. They all were smiling and in a very upbeat mood. I found it a little bit odd that no one had yet divulged the amount that had been raised.

I had a delicious dinner and after I finished I rolled over to the deck where my father-in-law was sitting.

"So Tommy," I asked him, "how did we do?" His eyes darted left and right, and he wouldn't look at me. I asked him again and got no answer. Finally, I started getting angry. "Tommy, how did we do? I have a right to know!" Instead of telling me he told me to guess. I thought he was breaking my balls. After all, for the 16 years that I was married to his daughter we had had a great relationship. He knew that I was a hard worker and that I had given his daughter a great life.

I started with the lowball amount. I knew the number was going to be huge, but I started with $200,000. He looked at me, put two thumbs up and motioned with his head and eyes for me to go up. So, I guessed $300,000, and was motioned up again. Well, $400,000 I guessed. Again he motioned to go up. Half a million dollars and again he motioned to go up. At this point his daughter, my wife of 16 years, came up from behind me and hissed into my ear.

"Get into the living room right now and wait for me." I had no idea what was going on and found myself blowing into the tube, turning away from my father-in-law, and rolling up the ramp into the house. She immediately came after me.

"Who the fuck do you think you are? I'll tell you what you have the right to know!" I sat in the chair in stunned disbelief. I was terrified. Was this really happening? I felt myself shrinking in the chair. I was alone, surrounded by the enemy, and in this case, the enemy was the person that I'd given every bit of my life to for sixteen years of blood, sweat, and tears

She told me to get in the van immediately, that I was going to be taken back up to the nursing home. I did what I was told. I rolled down the ramp of the deck not even able to say a goodbye to my sons. She drove the van, and I sat in my wheelchair in complete silence the entire 70 mile trip. When we arrived at Achieve, she put on an act as if nothing had happened. She sloughed off her verbal abuse of me, attributing the incident to stress. I said nothing as my therapists prepared me for sleep.

The next day, she was right back for my therapy session, acting as if nothing had happened. My Mom called during the week wanting to know how much money was raised by Keenan Strong. I told her "I don't know. I wasn't told." I left out the part that I had asked and was verbally abused in return.

For my part, I tried to put the Mother's Day 2014 terrifying incident in the past. I suppressed the memory of it to try to get through each day of therapy and the lonely hours leading to bed. Time marched on and May turned to June.

I had made it very clear that it was my intention to return to North Rockland High School to resume my teaching career in September of 2014. I organized a meeting with all the key players. My superintendent, assistant superintendent, high school principal, and the chair of the history department were present. They were open to the idea, and instead of telling me it was a bridge too far to cross, they asked me what I needed. The only glaring need that I could see was that I had to have a full-time teaching assistant in the room with me. I would need fingers behind the keyboard of the computer. Beyond that, I believed that I'd be able to do almost everything else independently.

After the meeting, I was confident that I would be able to return full-time in September, but a few days later I was notified that a "sick bank" was set up by everyone in the district, and they each contributed 1 day from their own personal sick days. Enough days were raised to buy me another year of salary and benefits until I was a little bit stronger. Then, I would be able to return full time in September of 2015. This was an amazing gesture of generosity on the part of my colleagues and of the whole district.

It was June, 2014, one full month after the Keenan strong fundraiser and I still had no idea how much money was raised or where the money was located. After the Mother's Day incident, I was simply afraid to ask.

June turned to July, and then a shock came. MVP, my insurance company through North Rockland High School, had given notice that I was to be put out of the nursing home in early July. My wife immediately launched into gathering forces at Achieve to fill out an appeal. I was not to come home in July. By this time, I had been there for so long, institutional living was becoming normal. At Achieve, I knew if I called out someone would attend to me. I didn't feel the same level of certainty about the prospect of coming home.

The money from Keenan Strong had been available for two months and yet no bathroom had been built in my home. You have to ask yourself, why not? My best friend Michael, a mechanical engineer, had drafted a plan for a beautiful accessible bathroom. Everything could be completed for a sum of $25,000. He presented this plan to my father-in-law, only to be put off. For some reason, the Nichols did not want to spend the money to build a bathroom. I always thought my stay in Liberty was only going to be a sub-acute step down for a month or two and that I would be home shortly, but I had already been there for five months.

The appeal was accepted, and a new date for my discharge was set for one month later, August 20th, 2014. There would be no getting out of it. The bathroom would have to be built, and I would have to be allowed to come home. It is with great difficulty that I write these words because I am forced to confront the truth. I should have been brought home two weeks after the fundraisers on May 3 and 4. Instead, I was left there for three more months. Three months of isolation, alienation from my sons, and loneliness. The loneliness that I felt is similar to watching a time-lapse of a beautiful green leaf. The leaf turns to bright red in the early fall, to yellow later in the fall, finally falls to the ground, becomes brown, dries up and is easily crushed beneath a footfall.

CHAPTER 10

A SORT OF HOMECOMING

On August 20th of 2014, I left the Achieve Nursing Home in Liberty, NY and returned to my home in New City, NY. I had been gone for 11 months.

Before I left, I asked if I could go in to speak to all my therapists during their lunch hour. I asked them to all gather in a circle and spoke to them for about five minutes. My remarks, while completely unrehearsed, came from the heart. For six months these people had treated me with great love and dignity. The equipment there was antiquated and minimal, but they made up for it with their enthusiasm and care. I had no idea at the time, but I was in a position where the right words came out of me. "Do me one last favor. Please don't ever get in your car to go home, not even once, thinking that you didn't have an impact. Every smile, every word of encouragement, every comforting touch enabled me to become stronger every day. After my talk to the therapists I wheeled out into the recreation room and there was a large cake waiting for me. Everyone, nursing staff included, was gathered to bid me farewell. Once again, I was called on to make some remarks. I tried to come up with a talk similar to the one I'd given to the therapists, but I fell short. One person that I would miss the most was my nurse's aide Trina, who was rough around the edges but had a heart of gold.

A month earlier I had attended the homecoming party for my friend Tony from Achieve. There were over seventy family and friends waiting to greet him when he arrived home, and they held a large party. Tony had been given a hero's welcome as he had also been gone for almost a year in rehab.

On the drive home, I remember feeling nervous. I did not know what the plan of care would be. As lonesome and depressing as the nursing home could be, I knew that there would be a nurse and a nurse's aide on call at all times. I was coming home, discharged into the care of my wife, a registered nurse. Unlike my friend Tony, I arrived home to no one. I had been gone almost a year and there was no one home to greet me, not even my sons.

Almost immediately after arriving home, I met the woman who would ultimately save my life. We were sitting on the back deck when I met Jane Kennedy. Jane had come to us on the recommendation of my cousin Mary Brady. Jane was married, and had two children in their late teens. We talked for a while with my wife indicating my needs and Jane's responsibilities. Jane said she would be honored to take the position. Her fee was only $10 per hour.

Jane, a stage four breast cancer survivor, took on my case. We were kindred spirits because, for some unknown reason, God gave us both a second chance. Jane was simply doing the most that she could with the time she had. I was not yet at that point. My insurance at North Rockland would cover a nurse's aide from 5 PM to 9 PM. Jane's job would be to help get me ready in the morning. My morning routine was an hour-long slog that included cleaning me if I had had a bowel movement during the night, getting me dressed, turning me in order to get the sling for the Hoyer lift under me, and then hoisting me into my chair. After that, it was down the hall into my gigantic bathroom.

The bathroom was built begrudgingly after insurance informed my wife that they would no longer pay for my stay in Liberty. Instead of the bathroom being built months before when my friend Mike drew up the plans, everyone was now called on to jump through hoops. My father-in-law was the supervisor on the job and now had to call in favors from everyone. Scotty Lauder did the plumbing; my brother-in-law did the electrical, and my friend Shaun McHugh did all the carpentry. The contractors, who donated their labor, had to work feverishly to get the structure built. The only cost my in-laws had to pay out of the Keenan Strong funds was for materials.

Jane and I would enter the bathroom and she would handle my personal hygiene. With great tenderness and care, she would apply a hot washcloth to my face before shaving me. This was a full-service salon. Jane would trim my nails, my nose hairs, and brush my teeth. As time went on, we would talk about life and just about everything. I felt safe and secure when I was with her. I knew that I could tell her anything and it would be kept in confidence.

My wife had purchased a new bed with an airflow pillow top mattress. The bed was queen-size so my wife and I could both sleep in it. The bed did have a feature where the top of the bed rotated up so I could sleep in a better position. I knew that there was going to be trouble when my wife, on the very first night, insisted that we sleep with the bed down, leaving me in an uncomfortable position. I'd spent the last 11 months sleeping in a bed in an inclined position. I had air conditioning at Achieve, but that was a no go at home; Meghan would only sleep in the warmth. Now, I suddenly found myself sleeping in a hot room, in an uncomfortable bed, with a woman who made it clear I was interfering with her comfort.

Thanksgiving

When the Thanksgiving holiday rolled around in November 2014, I knew better than to even mention the names of my brothers to my wife or her family. To do so was to court danger. My brothers, for their part, stayed away and avoided contact lest there be reprisals for me. My Mom was with me nearly every day and did everything in her power to keep the peace and not anger my wife. Far from it, she went above and beyond, taking me to nearly every medical or therapy appointment to try to make my wife's life a little bit easier.

When it came time to enjoy our meal, only the Nichols family was present. I sat in my wheelchair at the head of the table and called for quiet, as I wanted to say grace before the meal. I said a very heartfelt prayer of thanksgiving, looking around at each person at the table and thanking God for everything that they had done for me. It was late November, and I still did not know how much was raised by the Keenan Strong fundraiser in May. Seven full months had passed and no knowledge of the money was provided to me. As I look back on it now, it is clear that I was good-natured and trusting to a fault. I believed that everyone was like me, good in both heart and soul. How truly wrong I was! Thanksgiving dinner was delicious and my caregiver, Mary Ramos, arrived at 5 PM and, at 8 PM, she started to get me ready for bed.

Once I was settled in bed, the house phone rang. It was my younger brother John. My wife answered the phone, put it on speaker, and brought it back to me. I spoke with John for a few minutes, asking him about how everyone was doing. John was married to Denise and together they had four children. I didn't know where my wife was while I was having this conversation.

At the end of the call, John said, "I love you, Billy." I said "I love you John" right back. No sooner had the phone call ended than my wife stormed back into the room and started yelling at me. "You said you loved him? How could you, after the way he disrespected me?" She continued to bombard me with chastisements and a few expletives thrown in. I felt completely intimidated and helpless, laying there in bed without the ability to fight back. I told her I loved my brother and nothing she could do or say was going to change that.

I called my brother back and then had a five minute conversation about how he disrespected my wife. This is not how I felt. John showed absolutely no disrespect to Meghan, but my brother simply had stated the obvious months before, that my wife was damaged and seriously needed professional help.

During the time leading up to Christmas of 2014, my continued attempts to help Pat with his homework were met with failure after failure as I kept falling asleep while trying to help with his reading comprehension. Once again, my wife–the registered nurse, refusing to give me sleep medication–had set me up to fail. She would wake me up and continue to berate me

One night in early December, a knock came at the front door of our side hall colonial. On this particular night, I had fallen asleep during homework time and was the victim of a verbal assault once again. The knock at the front door was from my old friends, the Cooneys. Diane and Jackie Cooney were my neighbors when we grew up together on Jay Street in Stony Point. Jackie, Diane, and their children were out on the front lawn with Christmas carols blaring from an iPhone, and they were all singing along to the music.

I rolled my wheelchair to the edge of the open front door and watched and listened with a great big smile on my face. We exchanged greetings and I thanked them so much for coming down. They sang "Feliz Navidad" and two other carols. If I'd been in my right mind, I would've invited them in for hot chocolate and cookies and maybe a glass of wine for Jackie and Diane. However, having just come through a withering barrage of verbal assault, I didn't think that I could invite them in. My wife was sitting in the family room the whole time and did not come to the front door to see the caroling. When the Cooneys left, I rolled my wheelchair back into the family room and told her who it was and what was going on. She then asked me, "Why didn't you invite them in?"

I simply muttered, "I don't know."

How could I have invited these lifelong friends into the hell in which I lived? How could I try to put on a smiling, brave face? My wife had the ability to put on a smiling act, after immediately inflicting a verbal assault on a defenseless cripple, but I did not...

In early January 2015, my wife started to talk about going back to work on a part-time basis. I thought that this was a good thing. After all, in my mind, there was nothing that was going to stop me from returning to work even though I was 100% disabled. The outlet was going to be good for my wife.

It was also during this time that Meghan stopped sleeping in my room on the first floor. I was left alone in the room with a baby monitor to use if I needed assistance through the night. More and more, I was being made to feel like a true inconvenience, a pain in the ass for my wife. The baby monitor system had been used with great success while I was at the nursing home. One of the nurses aides kept the other monitor with her on her person at all times. This way, every time I called, I got an immediate answer. At home, it was a different story. My calls for help went frequently ignored and, over time, this scenario only increased. It is important to note that one of the main reasons for the Keenan Strong Fundraisers was to provide for a caregiver to stay with me through the nights and attend to these requests, but the money was never made available.

My habit of waking up at 3 AM in need of Xanax to get back down to sleep persisted. The problem now was that there was no one here to give me the medication so that I could get a decent night's sleep and be effective the next day. My wife refused to give me the Xanax.

During my many times in the car with my Mom, I tried to begin to explain what was going on within my home. Mom was a devout Catholic woman who always saw the good in people. She simply was not able to process, to get her head around, what was beginning to happen in my home. All she wanted to do was to lighten the load on my wife, take care of me, and make sure that the boys were okay.

Another Mother's Day

Mother's Day in 2015 was on Sunday, May 10th. On Wednesday of the previous week, with the help of one of my trainers from Push to Walk, I ordered a beautiful necklace as a present for my wife. Even though I knew things were not great, I still had hope. After all, she had been there through the whole first year right by my side. To the best of my knowledge, the necklace arrived on the day before

Mother's Day, but she never mentioned, and there was never a word of thanks.

A few years prior to my accident, Christmas 2008, I had a great idea. I went to Bourghol Brothers Jewelers in Congers and specially ordered a ring with the boys and my birthstones on a gold band. She opened up the ring and immediately said "I'm not going to wear that ring! You're making the decision that we're not going to have any other children!" I had no idea that the ring would be interpreted this way. It certainly was not my intention, despite the fact that I believed we would not be bringing any other children into the world given the fact that Pat's autism took a great deal of energy and time for both of us. The experience of having the ring thrown back at me caused me to say to myself, "I will never buy her another gift. But, of course, I did. After Mass that Mother's Day I went to lunch with my Mom and arrived home in the early afternoon to find my wife dressed to the nines. No sooner was I in the door when she packed up the boys and stormed out of the house, saying she was going to dinner with her family because I had not made any plans for her. I tried to explain that making plans for me was difficult, as I had no access to a phone and no ability to use my fingers on a keyboard, but she was already gone. Mom and I looked at each other. "What the hell just happened?"

By this time, Meghan was working three days a week. Aside from dispensing medication, helping Jane prepare me in the morning, and helping either Ketty, the agency aid, or Mary get me ready for bed at night, she had very little to do with me at all. I did not feel wanted in my own home. Communication between the two of us had all but broken down. Things were going from bad to worse and I didn't know how to stop it.

CHAPTER 11

FEELS LIKE "MISERY"

I wanted more than anything to take my sons to my niece Allison's high school graduation party on Saturday July 18th, 2015. Meghan was going to be away with her sister Theresa at a spa in Connecticut. During the week prior to the party, Meghan asked me if I was planning to go. I told her the restaurant is handicapped accessible and I really want Pat and Kieran to spend some time with their Keenan cousins. I was with Jane in my bathroom during this conversation. When Jane left, Meghan pounced. "How could you? You are condoning your brothers' disrespect of me. You are a bigger scumbag than your brothers." Ultimately the verbal abuse worked, and the next day I told my mother that we would not be able to attend the party. Meghan's mother ended up taking us to see the movie "Ted 2" in Nanuet. I sat in a darkened movie theater unable to laugh. I felt anger, rage, frustration, and a longing to be with my family that, for the time being, would remain unfulfilled. When Meghan returned, the mistreatment reached an all new level.

On July 21st, in the middle of the night, the fan that was used to cool the room shut down due to an electrical outage. A window air conditioner would have cost approximately $100, but I was not given one even though Meghan, who hated air-conditioning, no longer shared the room with me. I woke up soaked in sweat and saw the light on the baby monitor. I surmised that there was a power outage and that power came back, but the fan needed to be manually switched on. I started calling into the baby monitor in a normal speaking voice for roughly an hour. After that I was yelling at the top of my lungs. I was deathly afraid that the heat and my stress might bring about a stroke. Undeterred, I continued to yell at the top of my lungs, taking a break every few minutes. In my complete despair, I began to call out to my sons Patrick and Kieran, "Please help me!" Meghan appeared in my doorway at 7 AM. I had been awake since roughly 2 AM. She looked at me and said "What the hell were you screaming about?" I said "You heard me?" and she said "Yes, I heard you, but I wasn't coming down, I need my rest." I told her that I just needed two seconds for her to click the fan on, that's all I needed. I'll never forget her reply "Billy, you needed a fan? That's what you were screaming about? You weren't dying, stop your drama. Shut up and go back to sleep." She turned around, went back down the hallway, poured herself a cup of coffee, and waited for Jane. When Jane showed up, Meghan gave her a big smile, as if nothing at all had happened.

For the next ten days, I vehemently demanded to know about the Keenan Strong money. Each time, I was ignored. Megan continually responded to my demands with the answer, "I don't know how much was raised!" How could she not know how much was raised? I demanded to have a meeting of our two families in my home to finally get to the bottom of Keenan strong. She snapped at me, "There's not going to be any meeting of our families!" Like a dog with a bone, I simply would not let it go. In the kitchen one night during this 10 day battle, I was demanding to know about the money and my wife was standing over me and screaming, "You put yourself in that chair!" I did not know it at the time but my caregiver was in the family room and witnessed the exchange. That same night, my wife gave my caregiver a ride home and while in the car she said, "I'm sorry that you had to hear that. The money that Billy is arguing about is not for him. It's for me and the boys." (My caregiver divulged this information much later).

On Friday, July 31st Meghan was leaving for work and I demanded to know one last time. "This weekend, after Mary's wedding, we are going to sit down and have a phone call with your father, because I want to know how much money was raised, where it is, and how I can get access to it." I'll never forget her answer. "That money is not for you. That money is for me and my sons. You will never get a penny of it and I will burn it before you get it." With that she turned, left the room, and exited the house.

Saturday August 1st was the day of my cousin Mary's wedding to a great guy named Sal. They asked me to give the blessing before the meal, and I felt honored. On the way to the wedding, Meghan verbally abused me for the entire trip down to New Jersey. Because of Meghan's persistent attempts to keep me away from my brothers I had had little contact with them for almost a year, but I loved them, something she simply couldn't understand. In the midst of all this abuse, she told me we would be leaving as soon as I finished the blessing. I was up on the dance floor with one of the Cunningham brothers who held the mic while I gave the blessing. Meghan waited for me to leave. It would have been the perfect time to tell my family what had been happening. I was so beaten down, I rolled toward the door, and my brothers tried to follow. My mother got in the way of my brothers and told them not to go after me, once again trying to keep the peace. On the way home, the same abuse continued. "You're a disgrace as a husband and a father". We stopped to pick up Mary, my caregiver. Instantly Meghan put on her fake persona and gleefully told Mary what a great time we had had at the wedding.

The next day, my best friend Michael called to see if he could come take me out to dinner. I loaded up into the Popemobile and we rode up to the Hudson Water Club, a great pub and restaurant with a deck overlooking the Hudson River. We had dropped Kieran off at my brother Jim's house. This was the first chance that I had to fill in a non-family member about the abuse that was going on at home. To this day I still don't think that Mike fully understood the terror I felt in my own home. Maybe he thought it was a tad exaggerated. But this was no exaggeration. Everything, down to the dates, down to the words she spoke, was real.

After dinner, I asked Michael to take me to my brother Jim's house in Stony Point where Kieran was swimming with his cousins. No sooner had I arrived than I began telling Jim everything that had been going on in my house. I talked for an hour straight and then Jim, who was a retired NYPD officer and now in the security business, came out with a listening device. It had about 18 hours worth of life in it. It would fit right in the bottom of the wheelchair. I told him that I could not use it. If Meghan ever found it, I was afraid to imagine what she would do.

When Jim heard about the abuse and that Meghan had claimed the Keenan Strong money was hers, he almost went crazy. He wanted to go to the police. I was very unsure about this because I feared what she might do to me, so Jim scheduled a meeting for mid-August at the Center for Safety and Change, an advocacy group that was housed in the Rockland County Courthouse and advocated for abused spouses. By the time I went to the appointment at the Center for Safety and Change, the wound that had been diagnosed at Helen Hayes back in June as "having the circumference of a nickel and the depth of a mild abrasion" and "appears to be healing" had deteriorated rapidly.

The "mild abrasion, the size of a nickel" was being treated by my wife, until she left for vacation at the Jersey Shore in August. While my wife was away on vacation at my parents, Jersey Shore house, Jane was in charge of dealing with the wound. The first day she took a look at it, she looked me dead in the eye and said "Billy this is really, really bad". She took a cell phone picture of the wound and I nearly fell apart. What started as the size of a nickel with the depth of mild abrasion had deteriorated into a wound the size of a tennis ball with the depth all the way down to the tendon. Jane immediately texted this photo to my cousin Mary Brady, also a registered nurse. Mary alerted my family and rushed over. It was a medical intervention. Mary spent the next hour calling Nyack and Good Samaritan Hospitals. Mary got me enrolled in the Good Samaritan Hospital wound care program. Jane saved my life by alerting my family.

At the Center for Safety and Change, I was brought in to meet a social worker named Justine. My brother Jim and my Mom were present at the meeting, but this was a meeting that my Mom never should have attended. If she had not been there, I might have had the strength, given Jim's presence, to go to the Clarkstown police and report the abuse.

For one hour I spoke nonstop about everything that had been going on in my home. At the end of the hour, Justine looked at me.

"Bill, I'm going to tell you three things. Number one, you've been the victim of domestic abuse. Number two, your wife is going to divorce you. And number three, you should go to the police immediately."

Going to the police is exactly what I needed to do. It may have stopped my being victimized by Meghan and the Nichols family. But I didn't. What was wrong with me? Why did I listen to my mom? Why did I not go to the police? I was the victim of domestic abuse. I was the victim of financial fraud. I was a helpless, defenseless victim, and the Center for Safety and Change was empowering me; yet, I still refused.

There were several times in my life when I needed to be protected from myself, and this was one of them. By my not calling the authorities, Meghan continued to act without consequence. The absence of punishment is a reward. The lack of respect she had for me had built up over 16 years. She had no reason to think that I would ever rebel. As I write these words, I feel ashamed. How could a man who acted with such courage in his life be made to feel so diminished as a human being? As I look back in time, the abuse was always there. I was often made to feel guilty for the simplest of my life's pleasures. Whether it was surfing, going to see Jimmy Buffett, or wanting a new instrument, I was subject to Silences that could last weeks. I never knew when the next one would start. I spent 16 years tiptoeing through the minefield of the marriage doing everything in my power not to attract negative attention. In the absence of love, benign neglect would suffice. With all that was going on, in the deepest reaches of my mind, the following words represent exactly how I felt at the time:

I believed with every fiber of my being that this accident might not have happened if I had the strength to follow my convictions. In the summer of 2010, my marriage had become so broken and painful that I begged for marriage counseling, only to end up at counseling alone. I could have walked away from the marriage with a clear conscience. I stayed because I felt it would be selfish to take myself away from my sons. In reality, it would have been an act of self-preservation. After the failed attempt at marriage counseling, I did not continue in therapy. If only I had continued, I would have come to the realization that I had it within my control to break free. I would have found a place to live near my sons and been there for them every single day in their lives. At the same time, I would have found the love of a woman who shared my love of music, my love of the ocean, my love of triathlon, and the joy of surfing. In this way, I feel like I have failed and in doing so caused tremendous pain and suffering to my entire family.

Jim and I spoke about the merits of going to the authorities, but my Mom interjected. "We can't do that to the boys. They've been through a terrible trauma and this would only add to it." I love my Mom, but she was not there in the room to see who my wife truly was. She was not in the room when I begged for a fan. She was not in the room when I called out, hour after hour, at the top of my lungs, fearful that I would die of a stroke. She was not in the room when I asked for the money and was told that the money "is not for you; it's for me and my children!"

The meeting at the Center for Safety and Change was held in the middle of August and presented itself as the perfect opportunity to get me the help that I needed. But once again, I put the well-being of my children before my own. There was a huge difference this time around, however. This time, selflessness almost killed me.

The life that I had spent 16 years building was eroding right under my feet. It was obvious from the very beginning that I was not loved, just tolerated because I was a good provider. As I look back on it now it is quite clear that I was in an abusive marriage. My in-laws and my wife could never understand my joy because they lived their lives without any. Instead of going to the authorities, Mom and I continued to pray to end my suffering. On one of these trips to the noon Mass, my brother John joined us. By this point, I was attending mass every Tuesday and Thursday and my prayer was always the same. I was praying for deliverance from the darkness that enveloped my home. There is evil in this world that you cannot "pray away." The only way to stop what was happening would have been to go to the authorities with the charge of abuse of a disabled man.

There were three components to each visit to the shrine. The first was the liturgy, followed by the Holy Rosary, and then the Chaplet of the Divine Mercy. With John present during the Rosary, I asked the congregation. "Please pray for my wife. She suffers so greatly because of my injury."

At the end of the service my mom wanted to know. "Billy, what was that?" In my innocence, my naïveté, in my inability to see the truth right in front of me, I still prayed that things would come around. What I didn't know was that I was nearly done for.

My time at the shrine and my private counseling with Father Tom had brought me to the point where I was beginning to feel some true peace. I had begun to understand my suffering through the suffering of Christ. I didn't fully see it at the time, but in the suffering of Christ and my suffering there was an allegory. The halo that had been screwed into my skull after my injury was my crown of thorns. I had been betrayed by the closest person to me. Not only did her family let it happen, they were complicit in the entire conspiracy.

How was Jesus betrayed? He was betrayed with the kiss, and so was I. The feigned attention and affection in public was just a lie. What was Christ betrayed for? He was betrayed for 30 pieces of silver, and for what was I betrayed? I was betrayed for money. Nothing but blood money. My wife's family, every last one of them, wrote me off and discarded me.

At some point, a reasonable man or woman would think, "What are we doing? What we're doing is wrong." Their motive was a simple one. Billy Keenan was never going to walk again and he was never going to be able to work. The money had to be taken for the good of Meghan and the boys. All of the work that I'd done to build a life for their daughter over 16 years was forgotten in an instant.

At some point during that horrible summer of 2015 I said to my mother-in-law, "I feel that this is going to end in divorce."

She responded, "Meghan is just upset about a few things." What I didn't know, what I couldn't possibly know, was that the thing she was most upset about was that I was still alive.

Summer drew to an end and I prepared myself for the return to school. As of yet I did not know how I was going to be able to teach again, only that I had to. Throughout my life I had built up a reserve of resilience that always powered me through the toughest times. My return to teaching would be the next one. Not long after my injury, I made a promise to myself that I would return. I would do whatever it took to keep that promise.

Teaching high school history, even as an able-bodied man, is a difficult profession. You have to have complete command of the content, constantly be "on", and be able to keep the attention of a room full of 15-year-olds. My style of teaching was to be part Professor and part standup comic. I had always relied on humor to liven up even the most boring lessons. Now, as a quadriplegic, I could not rely on my sense of humor to carry the day. I was going to attempt something almost unthinkable, and I was going to do all of this without support on the home front. In fact, I had the exact opposite of support.

On Labor Day Monday, my wife invited Maria and Tony Martino to our house for a luncheon. Tony was a quadriplegic but still had more ability than I did. He had never been trached and vented, and had developed the ability to drive his own wheelchair with one of his hands. I truly had great affection for Tony. He was an Italian immigrant and a self-made man who worked as a contractor and a part-time driver at the local racetrack. Maria was always good to me and always brought me home cooked meals while I was at Achieve.

On this visit however, they were brought down for one reason: to get me to sign over the primary residence in New City and the investment property that we had purchased in Boynton Beach, Florida. Before the accident, the plan was to retire at age 55 with 25 years of service in the schools, sell the New City house, and buy a three bedroom condo in Ocean City, New Jersey. In this way, I could surf from spring to fall, and once October hit we could go to Boynton Beach, and I would surf the beaches of South Florida, all the while continuing my pursuit of being the Irish Jimmy Buffett.

After lunch, Maria started in on me. My wife was seated next to me and Tony sat on the other side of the table. The pressure to sign over the houses had started weeks before, but after the revelation of the stolen Keenan Strong money, I said nothing when the subject was brought up. I even went as far as calling the real estate attorney, Charles Davis, to find out if the properties were still in my name. This is how panicked and frightened I'd become.

Maria started telling us that the first thing they did after Tony's accident was to sign over all their properties to her. In this way, Medicaid would never be able to claim payment for services because Tony didn't own a thing. There was one huge difference between the Martinos and the Keenans: Tony had every reason to trust his wife. They had no idea of the abuse that I had endured all summer. They had no idea that my wife had actually told me that she had taken the money, and that it was not to be used for me. They had no idea that I had been left alone in the 95° room crying out all night for a fan. They were acting out of ignorance.

The more I resisted, the more I was silent in the face of this increasing pressure, the more vehement Maria became. Finally in exasperation she said something that I simply could not abide, "Your wife didn't have to bring you home. She loves you. This happened to her, as well. It wasn't just your life that was changed forever. It was her life too." Who did Maria think she was to tell me what to do? She and Meghan had mutually bonded over their shared miseries after meeting at Helen Hayes Hospital in 2013, and now Meghan was manipulating Maria to become her ally.

Wait a minute. My wife didn't have to bring me home? What the hell did that mean? I was always under the impression that my coming home was a when, not an if. Here was this woman telling me that my wife didn't have to bring me home. This was a home I built, a life I created by the sweat of my own brow. Who was Maria, sitting in my kitchen, telling me how to live my life? I wanted to scream at both of them to get away. The picture started to come into clarity. The only reason I was brought home from Liberty was because the insurance company refused to keep me there any longer.

After being attacked for well over an hour, I capitulated and agreed to sign over the properties. Mercifully, Tony and Maria left, and I immediately shifted all of my strength in body, mind, and spirit to the goal I had been working towards since November 2013 to return to the classroom...

Born Again

On Tuesday, September 8, 2015, I woke up at 5:30 AM. Teresa and Jane arrived at my door at 6:00 and started to get me ready. My wife took no part in the preparation.

I was dressed in a pair of khakis, a polo shirt, and the same shoes that I'd worn the last time I taught all the way back in September 2013. At 7 AM, I was at the end of my driveway waiting for the handicapped accessible Rockland County Trips bus to pick me up and drive me to school. Teresa and Jane were waiting by my side and my wife was there as well. When the bus arrived, the wheelchair lift was brought down to ground level and I slowly rolled the chair onto the lift, was belted in, and raised up into the bus. I moved slowly into position. The driver then clamped my wheels to the floor of the bus. My wife waved excitedly from the driveway and called out, "I love you!"

I love you? How could she say such a thing to me after everything that she had put me through? Words that should be comforting sounded unnatural. She was telling me she loved me! The memory of it is chilling and one that I absolutely repudiate with everything in me.

This woman who had conspired to take close to $1 million in Keenan Strong money, who had left me alone in a room in sweltering heat with wanton disregard, who verbally abused me on numerous occasions, and who ignored a dangerous stage four, life-threatening pressure ulcer, was telling me she loved me. It is a sickening memory.

The bus arrived at the Annex section of North Rockland High School at 7:20 AM. Waiting for me at the door was a lovely woman named Sue Segalbacher. Sue had volunteered to be my teaching assistant. As we made our way to the classroom we started to talk. After every couple of words I would have to blow into my sip and puff to continue the forward momentum down the long hallway towards room 504. Once we got to the room, Sue turned and looked at me. "Well, what do you need me to do?"

I immediately clicked into teacher mode. I started to go through the mental checklist of things that I would have to do to prepare for students later that day. Luckily, the school had given me the first period of the day free. That meant that Sue and I would be able to put our heads together each morning and prepare the day's lessons. The first day was all about filling out the students' information index cards. I would use these cards over the coming days to get to know each student one by one. This year, however, was very different. I had to address the elephant in the room, and the elephant was me.

A lot of the students, however, had absolutely no clue what they were walking into. I heard a number of them exclaim under their breath as they entered, "Oh Shit!"

After attendance was taken, I wheeled my chair to the front and center of the room. For the next 40 minutes, I told them my story. I held nothing back. I wanted to get everything out in the open and then take any of their questions. Some of the students had questions, and mostly they were about the wheelchair. I explained the sip and puff system to them, and they were amazed. This was the hard part. I would have to tell my story four more times over the course of the day. But with each class period, my anxiety level decreased.

My course load was as it had always been—three classes of Global 10th grade history and two Psychology classes. The Psych electives were both junior and senior classes. I loved teaching Psych. The difference between sophomore and junior year is absolutely huge. The level of maturity and the amount of dialogue between teacher and student increase exponentially in the span of one short year. But I also loved teaching Global 10. I fought hard to blast through some of the more boring topics, to leave plenty of room for the topics I loved, the World Wars and the Cold War.

On that day, in the middle of the day around noon time, my wound VAC began beeping. The pressure ulcer on my right calf that was detected when Meghan was away in August was so severe that it needed a device called a wound VAC to begin the healing process. A wound VAC is a device that literally sucks out the dead tissue and brings forward the healthy granulated tissue needed to close the wound. This particular pressure sore was so deep that it would require five years to close. The beeping indicated that the wound VAC's battery needed to be charged. Holy crap, I thought to myself. I had Sue text my wife that I needed the cord to charge the battery so I could teach the remainder of the day. Amazingly, my wife responded very quickly and showed up with the cable. I did, however, have to endure a full class with my alarm beeping. I wanted the earth to open up under me and suck me into it. I was embarrassed, and I felt crippled.

During lunch, Sue walked with me to the elevator to get me to the main high school building. Once we got in the elevator, Sue said to me, "I think we're doing pretty good so far. We'll be just fine." We motored down the hallway of the main building to get my catheter bag drained by the school nurse, a really nice woman named Peggy.

Sue then took me to the Social Studies office so I could have a visit with all my friends. The problem was, nothing was the same. I had been gone for two full years. I tried to insert my two cents into each conversation, but it wasn't the same. I would continue to go to the office every day for about a month. After that I remained in my room and Sue remained in the classroom with me.

As I look back on it now, it was obvious that no one believed that I would be able to pull this off—even with the help of a teaching assistant. The teacher who substituted for me during my two year absence was standing ready in the event I was unable to carry out my duties as a teacher. What no one would've counted on was the fire that burned inside me to get back to life. I never forgot Steven McDonald's words. I needed to reclaim one shred of the life that I knew. I needed to establish myself as a man with dignity. I would not give up, there would be no retreat and no surrender.

My two best friends, Billy Robbins and Brian Diglio were frequent visitors to room 504. I relied on them heavily for help getting Sue up to snuff on the computer. Here's an obvious question. How does a man who cannot move his arms or legs teach high school history? The best way that I can answer this question is that I relied on Sue in much the same way that Tony Stark relied on Jarvis in the Ironman movies.

When Sue and I first started to work together, I would direct her. "Get chapter 17 section 1 PowerPoint." Something I should've done years before when I was able-bodied was take all of my PowerPoints and all of my Microsoft Word documents (tests, quizzes, and worksheets), and put them into corresponding computer files with chapter titles. Billy Robbins helped me do this one afternoon during the first week of classes. From 1996 to 2013, I had amassed a large backlog of tests, quizzes, and worksheets that I had created myself. For every section of every chapter in my text, I had written a corresponding PowerPoint with class notes. The able-bodied me would be able to move about the classroom, crack jokes, and keep the ball rolling, keep the students interested and employ humor. I would have no such ability in this wheelchair. Sue became not only the perfect teaching assistant but also a true partner in helping me to achieve my goal of teaching again. My pride was such that I would not allow myself to go back to school as a sideshow or charity case. Sue was there to help me in any way she could, and she did. We worked together to figure out how best to test the students. Each test was based on one chapter in the text. There would be 25 to 30 multiple-choice questions followed by an essay or written response. Multiple-choice were easily handled with the use of the Scantron sheet and the written response portion of the tests were all completed using a Chrome book laptop computer. The computer department was kind enough to give me the use of a cart with 30 laptops for the entire school year. The students wrote their essays in Google Docs and sent them to my Dropbox account.

On all of my free periods, instead of going to the nurses office to drain my catheter, Sue took over that responsibility. She would also eat her lunch very quickly and come back to help me grade my essays. For essays, Sue would sit at the computer and pull up each essay individually. I would recline in my wheelchair with my feet up to attempt to relieve the terrible pain of neuropathy in my lower legs that was part of my daily life. I'd read each essay on the SmartBoard. After a few tests, I made the process even easier by using the Regents rubric to formulate my comments. The students were provided a list of comments that were numbered, and at the side margin of each essay the students read the number for the comments. There was no playbook for bringing a quadriplegic back into the classroom, so we had to write our own. By the end of the first quarter, it was clear that this experiment, this impossible dream, was going to work. I was back!

Bloody Sunday

On Sunday, September 12th, I came home from Mass and my wife cornered me in the kitchen. She had set up an appointment with the estate lawyer on September 14th, the two year anniversary of my accident. My wife sat at the kitchen table going over the worksheet for our wills. I sat there and listened to my will being read. I wanted to scream, to run away, to be rescued. All of my earthly possessions would be going to my wife. "There's only one thing left to do," my wife said when she had finished reading the will. "On September 14th, we have to go see Charles Davis and you're going to sign over the two houses to me." She said that since the plan to go back to work would likely fail, we needed to get the properties out of my name so Medicaid would not force us to sell the houses.

I never really understood the ins and outs of Medicaid. It was never a thought in my mind that I would fail at work. I never had a moment of doubt that I couldn't pull off this miracle. For a long time, I sat silent. Then, after a long pause, I somehow found the will to fight one more time. "I understand the need to protect the assets," I said, "but I would feel a lot better about signing over the houses, if you would just tell me how much was raised by Keenan Strong."

Her response was to yell at me, "Oh no! You do not get to set conditions. You have to do this, you owe it to your family after what you did." The thing that I did, the crime that I committed that had me banished like Edmund Dantes to the Château d'If, was that I went surfing, got hurt, and ruined her "perfect little life". Five seconds passed before the next words out of her mouth told me all I needed to hear. "If you don't sign the houses over to me, I will file for divorce." I realized at that moment that it only took five seconds to go from the request to sign to the threat of divorce. Everything was clear to me at that moment. Even if I signed over the houses to her, what was to stop her from immediately filing for divorce? I realized then that if I took the pen in my mouth to make my mark I would be homeless, penniless, and childless.

This chapter derives its title from the film adaptation of the Stephen King novel, *Misery*. The movie tells the story of novelist Paul Sheldon, rescued from a car crash by one of his biggest fans, former nurse Annie Wilkes. Sheldon is subject to the most horrific treatment as he becomes a prisoner to Annie. He is literally in a fight for his life, cut off with no phone or way to signal for help. I would have a very difficult time watching this film. Although the incidences of abuse are in the past, the devastation lasts a lifetime. Writing this chapter took me back to some of the darkest days of my life. I took the most care in writing this chapter because there are many lessons to be learned from my experience.

If you find yourself in a toxic relationship, no matter the circumstances, get out immediately! There is nothing that you can do, nothing that you can give, that will ever change the person causing you pain. Please learn from the mistakes that I made. If you find yourself a victim of genuine abuse, contact the appropriate authorities and get the help that you need! Find the strength to advocate for yourself! In my case, I was strong enough to take the abuse but not strong enough to execute my escape. My escape should have occurred while I was still able-bodied. It's never too late to free yourself, until it is too late! My prayer is that this chapter will empower you to save yourself for those you love and those who love you.

CHAPTER 12

UNRECOGNIZABLE

After my bedtime routine on September 13th, I was settling down watching TV in the dark. Without any warning, my wife appeared like a specter in the doorway of my room. She wanted to know once and for all if I was going to sign. She then spat out the most chilling words that I had heard in that summer of darkness.

"This is not about love, or marriage, or kinship, or anything. This is what you owe your family." She pressed me once again, "Are you going to?" I said nothing. After a few more seconds she turned and walked away. My son Kieran had come down to say good night to me. I asked him to tell his mother to come back down. I was so beaten, so isolated, so alone, that I mumbled my acquiescence to the horrible request to sign over both houses. Darkness had truly descended upon my home.

I lay awake that long horrible night. My mind was racing as I was putting all the pieces together. I had just gone through eight months of verbal abuse, and now knew for sure that the Keenan Strong money was not going to be used for my care. My mind went back to the conversation on Sunday. It took her five seconds to threaten divorce if I did not sign. I lay awake all night formulating a plan.

Tuesday, September 14th, my two aides Teresa and Elma arrived to get me ready for school. At 7 AM, I was just finishing breakfast, getting ready to roll down the ramp to the driveway onto the Rockland County Trips bus to make the trek to North Rockland High School. My wife was sitting at the kitchen table drinking coffee waiting to question me.

"What time should I pick you up to go to the estate lawyers?" With my two caregivers by my side I knew that I was safe. I said that I was not going to the appointment and that I would come home on the Trips bus. I called my mom when I got to school and had her ready to meet me in the driveway when I got home that afternoon. The phrase from the great Roman orator Cicero rang true: "Alea iacta est"- the die is cast!"

After I refused to take my name off the deeds of the New City house and the Florida house, it was quite clear that my marriage was over. Things were so bad, so tense, that I was afraid to ask my wife for lunch money. One morning during that first week back in class, I called my son Kieran into my bathroom. I asked him in a whisper. "Could you go up to your room and bring down $20 from your piggy bank?" My wife was waiting right outside the doorway and as soon as Kieran had left the bathroom, she interrogated him to find out what I wanted. She degraded me once again, saying how pathetic I was that I had to ask my son for lunch money.

On Sunday, September 19th, I went to Mass at St. Francis of Assisi in West Nyack. I always loved spending time with my pastor, Father Rob McKeon. Father McKeon had spent every Thursday with me at Helen Hayes. My Mom dropped me off at home after Mass and my wife was sitting on the couch in the family room. I wheeled over to her and she didn't look up once from whatever magazine she was reading.

"I have a question," I said. "Do you want to continue in this marriage?"

She looked up at me and responded, "No." I asked if she had a lawyer and she said, "No." I told her I did. That was the end of the conversation.

Jim enlisted our uncle, Kevin, a retired NYPD detective, to help us in our search for justice. We started to meet regularly, trying to find out how much money was raised and exactly where it was. The truth is, we were all reeling. We were dealing with domestic abuse, verbal abuse, psychological cruelty, and financial fraud.

With all this turmoil in the darkness that was engulfing my personal life, the one bright spot was getting up every day and getting on that Trips bus at 7 AM. I was alone with my thoughts and could focus all my energy on getting through the day. I had to completely compartmentalize my grief, my pain, and my anger. I had to wipe all these emotions from my mind, shove them into a box, and tape it shut. I simply could not let them bleed out into the classroom.

As Sue and I got more friendly, I began to talk to her about what was going on in my personal life. She, like almost every rational person in my life, had difficulty wrapping her head around exactly what was happening. Again, I talked to my friends Brian and Billy about what I was going through and everyone was a little incredulous. However, they knew me to be an honest man, not given to lie.

She Washed Her Hands of Me

On Monday, October 3rd, at approximately 5 PM, my Mom and I arrived home from a doctor's appointment. I rolled up the ramp and into the kitchen with Mom behind me. My wife was sitting at the kitchen table with every bottle of medication that I was using. She also had the pillboxes lined up on the kitchen table.

"You need to learn how to fill Bill's pillboxes now. I'm no longer doing it." said Meghan addressing my mother. We were both completely blindsided. After all, she was a registered nurse. Even if she hated me and wished me gone, there should've been some continuity in care. My mother had no medical experience. Without a word, Mom sat down dutifully to learn how to fill my pillboxes.

Later that evening, my son Kieren had a Fall baseball game. My wife went to the game and arrived home at approximately 8:30 PM. My Mom stood up and got ready to go home.

122 The Road To Resilience

My wife then looked at her and said, "Where are you going, Eileen? Who is going to give Billy his night medications?"

Mom answered, "I thought you were."

My wife said in reply, "I told you already. I'm not having anything more to do with Billy's care."

My mother began to raise her voice, saying, "What are you doing? Are you stepping back completely?" My Mom was heated now.

In reaction, my wife, with the tone of her voice pure hatred, uttered this reply. "I told you. I'm not having anything more to do with his care."

I then turned to my mother and said, "Mom, call Barbara Keenan because I need someone with me in the room all night. I no longer feel safe in my home!" Mom got on the phone with my Aunt Barbara (a retired registered nurse) immediately, and Barbara packed a few things and came down. She slept on an inflatable mattress right next to my bed and I slept fitfully, traumatized by everything that had happened.

My eyes opened wide at 5 AM and I called out to my aunt saying, "Barbara, can you please go get me the phone?" She got the phone and I told her to call my in-laws at their house in Pearl River.

My mother-in-law picked up the phone and sounded deeply distressed. "What's the matter? Is everything okay?"

"Everything is not all right. I want to know right now how much money was raised by the Keenan Strong fundraiser!"

Try to imagine that you are me having this conversation. There was an incredible coming together and outpouring of love and support by a community that didn't know what else to do in the face of such tragedy. I had already been told by my wife that I was to be blamed for the accident, that the money was never mine, and that it was meant for her and my children.

Now, on a Monday morning in October, my mother-in-law gave this answer: "Why do you need to know? Aren't your needs being met?"

I yelled into the phone. "No! My needs are not being met. Your daughter will no longer be participating in my care! So things are not okay! Tell me right now, how much was raised by Keenan Strong?"

Again she started stammering, answering each of my questions by asking why I needed to know. After about five minutes, she switched tactics, saying that this was between me and my wife.

I answered again. "No no no! This is not between me and my wife. She won't tell me so you're going to tell me right now!" On the other end of the phone all I got was silence. I kept up my fight. Despite my threats to go to the authorities, she would not tell me.

When my Mom arrived at the house later that day to get me off the Trips bus at 3 PM, my father-in-law was already there doing yardwork.

He immediately began to yell at her, talking about her disgraceful son, who called them up at 5:30 in the morning. My Mom was blindsided. She had no knowledge of my early morning strike. The man who took the abuse all throughout his married life, that man who could not stand, finally stood up for himself. I would not let their treachery continue. The battle lines were clearly drawn.

This was the last straw, and there would be no coming back from it. The Keenan family was now at war with the Nichols. At this point, very few people knew what was going on in my home. I had not yet gone public or gone to the authorities and pressed criminal charges, which should have been my first move. To go the route of divorce litigation first was a fatal error. We were all feeding off each other's anger and indignation, and that was exactly what the lawyers loved. They take your emotions and stir them up even worse than they were, all the while racking up billable hours. I don't know if there is a lower form of scum on the planet than divorce lawyers. While I was in the ocean, bleeding from wounds both literal and figurative, the sharks were circling, taking small bites in succession. These sharks live on the money they take from people like me.

How Am I Supposed to Pay For a Divorce?

In the middle of October I made two phone calls that shocked even me. By this point, I was well used to having my whole world turned upside down. The injury was the least of it. The betrayal was the devil that I fought every single day.

Jim informed me that there was a PayPal account that was used by Keenan Strong to sell my CD, T-shirts, and wristbands. The account had approximately $50,000 in it. I called Pat, the bass player from Celtic Cross and an integral member of the Keenan Strong Committee, and told him, "Pat, Meghan and I are getting divorced and I don't have any money to pay for a lawyer!"

Pat wanted to know what the hell had happened. So I told him that I had not been given access to the Keenan Strong funds and had no idea how much money had been raised. Pat then told me something that left me in complete shock. He told me that he was in the car and wanted to pull over because he felt sick.

"Billy, I talked to Theresa a week after the events and asked her what the number was. She told me $750,000 and counting." The fundraiser had taken place one year and seven months prior and this was the first time I had heard an approximate number! I knew it had to be a number in excess of $500,000, but had no idea that it was close to $1 million.

Pat gave me the password to the PayPal account and with Jim's help we were able to get control of $55,000 from PayPal. Seeing that the money had been taken out of the account, Theresa went back to PayPal and got control of the $55,000. It was only with the help of Pat and a PayPal representative that we were able to get back the $55,000. We had now stumbled into the minefield of cyber warfare.

I made another phone call to a musician named Ken who had worked on the Keenan Strong committee. He told me the exact same information that Pat had told me, and that he contacted Theresa and pleaded with her saying, "Don't cause another tragedy." Theresa responded, "I don't know why people are so upset with an action they knew we were going to take." The Nichols believed that the money raised was meant for Meghan and the kids."

At this point, I became convinced that certain members of the Nichols family had conspired for months to collect and control the Keenan Strong funds. The Nichols were far ahead of all of us and we desperately tried to play a game of catch-up to no avail.

The Autumn of 2015 saw my family disintegrate before my eyes. Patrick's autism granted him a blissful oblivion to the horrors that were unfolding at our home. Kieran, unfortunately, understood that there was darkness descending on our once happy home. More and more, we had conversations in my bedroom before he retired for the evening. When he was laying in bed with me, it was clear that he was taking my side. It was during one of these talks that he revealed to me something he had seen in my bedroom upstairs .

"Dad, there is a security camera outside the bedroom you used to share with mom and a deadbolt lock is on it. I know I wasn't supposed to be in that room, but once when I went in to talk to mom, I saw a big safe in your old closet." Meghan was probably keeping the money there all along. This was a horrible situation for a 13-year-old kid to face. All he had known up until that point was a stable, happy family. Whatever else had transpired between my wife and me, we had kept him blissfully unaware. There is no doubt that my injury, coupled with the domestic difficulties, left him struggling to make sense of this world and to find a way to cope.

The Missing Pill

Meghan insisted she'd found a Xanax on the floor in my new quarterson the first floor, blaming my mother whom she forced to handle my medication. She then demanded that no one go upstairs to retrieve the medication. She didn't want anyone near the money, which I believed was in the safe that Kieran saw. Behind my back, she had contacted my best friend Michael and had him purchase a large safe that would be installed on the first floor of our house to contain all medications. Michael came over to the house with this massive safe and put it in the hallway closet. My wife then tried to compel my mother to get on her hands and knees and learn how to open the safe.

I had finally had enough and started to scream. "No Mom! You are not getting on your knees to open that safe!"

Michael sat at the kitchen table with Meghan while I was also in the kitchen. Michael expressed aloud his concern about our marriage, but he did not know that the marriage was already over. I said nothing. Meghan told him that I believed that there was a huge sum of cash in the house and she had no idea what I was talking about. I reminded her of what her father had said on Mother's Day of 2014 and the guessing game he'd played with me. Meghan claimed that he was not motioning for me to go up but rather shrugging because he didn't know the amount. Lies upon lies. I ultimately had Michael return the safe and the medications were kept in my bedroom closet.

What I kept coming back to was this question: the fundraising concerts had been held in 2014 and it was now the fall of 2015 and I still had no idea how much money had been raised or where it was. After Michael left, I remember screaming at my wife. "I'm not afraid of you anymore! Your reign of terror is over!" If I'd only spoken these words years earlier, I might have found the all-too elusive happiness. This remains one of my deepest regrets as I write this book.

It was right in the middle of this intense hostility that a man from Bullet Security arrived. I was now sitting outside on this beautiful fall day. He looked at me in the wheelchair and said, "I'm really sorry." I smiled and answered, "It's not your fault." I had no idea why he was there. I rolled in from the driveway, came into the kitchen, and saw the man installing a security camera in the family room. That meant that there was a security camera outside the master bedroom where the safe was kept and a security camera watching me and any visitors in the family room. One of the divorce lawyers whom we consulted strongly suggested that my brothers go upstairs, pry open the master bedroom door and take the safe. He looked me dead in the eye and said, "Mr. Keenan whatever is in that house is still technically yours!" I shook my head vehemently and said that there was no way that we could do such a thing. The bottom line was that I was still absolutely terrified and traumatized.

This was utter madness. I had adapted to being a prisoner in my own body. I was now a prisoner in my own house, with no privacy to boot.

How to Compartmentalize for Dummies

I had survived my "death", regained my breath against all expert medical opinions, somehow managed to leave the nursing home after six long months still intact, and lived through abuse and neglect that left me questioning whether God was still with me. The only saving grace at this point in my life was that I found joy in being with my students every day. The conversations, the arguments, all of it. Hell, even having to throw students out of class, it was all fun.

Mr. Montero, Dr. Gill, and most of the other assistant principals would occasionally stick their heads into room 504. Each time, they found me teaching, sitting in the middle of the room in my wheelchair, doing my thing.

What I want my story to say is that even in the midst of all of these horrible things, nothing can triumph over the human spirit. I wanted to teach. I needed to teach. I want people to understand that even though you may be beaten down and crippled whether in body or spirit, you can still turn around and claim victory. At this point in my journey I did not know of Dr. Viktor Frankl or his great work, *Man's Search for Meaning*. Frankl somehow survived the horrors of the infamous Nazi concentration camp at Auschwitz and wrote an unforgettable memoir of his time there. He had a unique sensibility as a trained psychiatrist living through the Holocaust. He endured unspeakable cruelty from his captors and also witnessed incredible acts of compassion, generosity, and courage from his fellow inmates. Perhaps his most important message was that even in the most horrible of circumstances, the last freedom we all have that nobody can take away is our choice of attitude, deciding how we will meet whatever life throws our way.

I did everything in my power not to let my domestic problems bleed over into the classroom. Every once in a while, however, the kids would ask about my wife, to which I'd respond, "I'm getting a divorce."

On a trip to the nurse's office to empty my catheter bag, I learned that the mother of my former girlfriend Sara was substituting for the school nurse (Sara was the girl for whom I left the Army back in 1992). I greeted her and she asked how everything was going.

"My wife is divorcing me. I guess it's not a lot of fun being married to quadriplegic."

A Bridge Too Far

I remember the day that my Mom became my primary caregiver. By late September I was pleading with her to stay with me through the night. At that point, she did not truly understand the horror that I'd been living through. She could not get her head around what was going on all through that summer of 2015. How could she? How could anyone in their right mind understand what was going on? It defied understanding.

Mom and I lived our lives in the light, surrounded by good people. Our experience with deceit and greed was limited. My father, had he been alive, would've seen through it all. He would never have let my wife and her family get away with what I came to believe was abuse and fraud. Everything would've been on the up and up because my father would have taken charge– quietly and gently commanding respect.

From October 4th on, my Mother was with me from the moment I arrived home from school through the evening hours. Most nights she slept by my bedside on an inflatable mattress. My Keenan cousins formed a roster, taking time away from their busy lives with their families to relieve my Mother and stay by my bedside. When my cousins took a part in my care, Meghan was forced to curb her behavior. She advised all of my cousins that there was an alarm on the side entrance door and gave them the code. She warned them that if the wrong code was entered and the alarm sounded the $90 penalty would have to be paid by the Keenans. This is how crazy she was. It was as if she knew the price of everything and the value of nothing.

On the night of my 30th high school reunion in November 2015, my boys had just gotten back from the Army Football game at West Point where they had a great time with many of their cousins.

As I was getting ready to be picked up for my reunion, Meghan began asking Pat how much he had to eat. Were there any problems? Were you ever hungry? Did anything go wrong? Did you feel uncomfortable? I knew what she was doing and I became enraged, screaming at her, "Stop your crap! I know what you're doing. There was nothing wrong and he had a great time so leave it be!" She was trying to get Patrick to say that he was treated badly and that he didn't get enough to eat. When Pat is too hungry, he often would have a meltdown. I believe that his mother was trying to get him to meltdown so she could blame it on the Keenan's. I'd been watching TV while all this was going on. When she got in the way of the TV, I inched my wheelchair closer to her, telling her to back up. She refused. This was as close to an all out brawl as we had ever had. Thirty minutes later, Mike arrived to take me to the Reunion. He walked in and he could sense the tension in the room. Everyone was sitting in the family room and I was waiting with my jaws clenched.

Mike walked in and stared. Before he had time to greet everyone, we were out the door and in the car. I told him what was going on. He listened to me and acknowledged that it was clear that things were as bad as they could possibly get. How wrong he was.

By the time I got to the reunion I realized that my being there was a complete mistake. I felt out of place. My emotions were so raw that I was telling people–classmates of mine that I hadn't seen for years–everything that was happening.

"My wife has taken all of the Keenan Strong money!"

"I need help, I'm being abused!"

"What am I going to do?"

It was all coming out of me and I sounded like a complete lunatic. Who could believe this? Who could possibly understand what was going on? My classmate, Ellen Galvin, just said "No worries Billy we'll organize another benefit." By 9:30 PM, I was begging Mike to take me home. I spent the whole way home from Pearl River apologizing.

In November, when the rain was lashing down one day, my Mom met me at the driveway with a big umbrella upon my return from school. We headed to the back door as quickly as we could in the rain, but the wind was fierce, battering us as we moved up the driveway onto the ramp. We got to the sliding glass door on the deck and there was Meghan, no more than 10 feet away, sitting on the couch in the family room playing with her phone. We knocked on the glass door and she didn't move–no response. We began banging on the glass door. She simply waved her hand, mouthing to my mother, "Go around, Eileen!" My Mom covered me with the umbrella and told me to wait. Mom, 72, jogged down the ramp, entered through the side entrance, walked through the house, and let me in through the back door on the deck.

When I got inside, I stared at her. "Have you no shred of humanity left?"

She looked up from her phone and said calmly and condescendingly, "I don't know what you're so excited about. Why are you so angry?"

The Last Family Outing

On the day of Patrick's Confirmation at St. Francis of Assisi in West Nyack, I was anticipating driving to Church with my mother when Meghan announced that morning, "I'm driving. We are going to this as a family. It is the last event we will be attending as a family."

When there was so much hatred and ill will in the house, why on earth would we even bother to go through the charade of traveling together? To this day I have no explanation for her decision. Regardless of my feelings, my aides got me dressed and I got in the van with Kieran, Pat, and Meghan.

Kieran had already chosen the Keenan side and the Nichols family viewed him with the same seething anger they projected towards me. All the seats in the church were taken when we arrived, so we found spots in the opening by the church hall. I watched in silence as all of my in-laws filed in one by one. I wanted to scream and run them over with my chair, but I held my tongue throughout the ceremony.

Confirmation is one of the most beautiful sacraments in our church, where after years of education in the pursuit of Christ, we open ourselves to accept the gift of the Holy Spirit. These people, whom, I believe, wished for my demise, were sitting there in a Catholic Church looking like normal, upstanding, and moral people. It was the only time in a Catholic Church when I felt the absence of God. I saw only blood and felt only anger at their betrayal. I can't sugarcoat it. They had no idea how far I would be willing to take the fight.

After the ceremony, Meghan announced that we would be going to lunch at *Joe and Joe's* in Pearl River. We sat at a table in the restaurant and spoke not one word to each other. The boys ordered chicken fingers and fries, and I had a steak with some vegetables. Meghan cut the steak and fed me in silence. There was not one hint of joy, but we got the luncheon out of the way for the sake of appearances. The ceremony at church was over. This luncheon was completely unnecessary and actually quite cruel. Afterwards, Kieran and I were taken home and dropped off under my Mom's care before Patrick and Meghan departed for the Nichols' in Pearl River.

What amazed me most was the lack of shame that these people exhibited by walking into church with their heads held high. When I asked for the money back on October 4th, my mother-in-law

Margaret questioned why I needed to know that information. I asked again and she still wouldn't tell me. To me, they were all ruthless dissemblers in private, while to the outside world they appeared to be caring and honest.

I believe Meghan meant to have that wound grow and to become infected—how could a registered nurse not realize how serious it was? My brothers insisted that she was only a short time away from putting the pillow over my head. It would've been the perfect crime. Respiratory failure would be an easy explanation. There would be no witnesses.

Thank God that my Mom and the Keenans intervened on my behalf. We used to sing a hymn in my Catholic grammar school that went like this: "Whatsoever you do to the least of my brothers, that you do unto me". Did God feel all of my pain as they committed their sins? Does God react when hypocrites walk into His house as if they are righteous and just people. I am asking the unknowable.

CHAPTER 13

BILLABLE HOURS

Shortly before Thanksgiving I arrived home from Mass on Sunday and found my wife and her sister with all my instruments and equipment laid out. They were cataloging each piece of equipment by make and model. They intended to sell off each piece as they were considered "marital assets". I argued vehemently against this. "These things are not marital assets. I worked a job for 16 years and gave you every penny. That should be enough." Then Meghan tried to twist my words against me asking, "How many years did you work? How much money did you make?" I said, "You know damn well how long I worked and that I gave you every penny, keeping nothing for myself. These instruments have nothing to do with you; they are not marital assets; these pieces of equipment are all my possessions!" Still they continued with their cataloging.

I couldn't help but think of the image of Christ and his crucifixion when Roman soldiers stripped him naked and gambled for his clothes. The Keenan Strong money was not enough for my wife and her sister. They had to come for the last bit that I had left. I hated them both. There seemed to be no end to their hostility toward my survival and continued existence. We suspected that Theresa had been the orchestrator of the Keenan Strong theft and was therefore the enforcer behind what I call the family conspiracy. Maybe Theresa was not the brains of the operation, maybe that was Meghan all along. Or maybe it was the parents. I will never know.

I can only wonder if they ever questioned what they were doing. Did they ever question the morality of their actions? It seems they never did! Or did they just think they were doing what was right for Meghan and the boys? I think they felt that I had done this to myself and deserved the consequences.

During the first week of December 2015, I started to experience shortness of breath. I was coughing and unable to expel mucus. I thought I had the problem under control and went back and tried to teach. I knew something was wrong, but I couldn't put my finger on it. One night, when I was getting ready for a shower, I was rolled over on my side and went into immediate respiratory failure. I croaked out, "Roll me over! Roll me over, please, roll me over!" I was rolled over onto my back and regained my breath. My aide told my Mom to call 911.

I was rushed to Good Samaritan Hospital. An x-ray soon revealed that there was a plug of mucus lodged in my lung and that my right lower lung had completely collapsed. They attached me to a BiPAP machine to keep me breathing, but thankfully I was not intubated. My brother Jim and my Mom were with me in the emergency room and I remember Jim crying, calling out to God to let me live.

I was admitted to the hospital and spent the next few days trying to expel this plug of mucus. I was given frequent nebulizer treatments as the nurses tried to snake a tube down my nose and pull out the mucus, but my condition didn't improve. Finally the pulmonologist said what I'd been fearing.

"We are going to perform a bronchoscopy. I'm going to snake a tube down your nose into your lung and suck out the mucus." I was scared. He informed me that I was going to be intubated for the procedure and given a mild anesthetic.

Before the bronchoscopy, while I was gasping for air, the lawyers arrived in my room with my brother Jim. They wanted to go over the timeline of my abuse while I lay in bed trying to contribute whatever I could to the conversation. In reality, I was gasping for air. Even with all of this going on, the lawyers kept talking. I felt like

I was dying right in front of them and they still kept talking. After about an hour, they realized that I was not fit to continue. In the face of all of the abuse and the theft of the Keenan Strong money, the lawyers decided I should be the one to file for divorce. Shortly after the procedure, I was laying in bed resting comfortably when my Pastor, Father McKeon, arrived in my room.

I was delighted to see him—he had been such great counsel to me and got me to understand in the early days after my accident that I had a role to play. He was a man of spiritual contemplation and action. He was a true priest. He anointed me with the Sacrament of the Sick and we prayed and talked for a while. While we were talking, my mother-in-law walked into the room. She looked like she saw a ghost when she saw Father McKeon ministering to me. Without saying a word, she left an envelope at the foot of the bed and walked out. Father Rob and I looked at the envelope. I asked him to read the letter which was from Meghan.

It started out like this:

"Dear Billy,

I hoped we could come to an amicable divorce..."

After that, the letter went on for another two pages telling me everything that I had done to cause the divorce. There would be no amicable divorce. Had she said she was sorry, that she had to move on, and offered to share the Keenan Strong monies and co-parent—that would have been an amicable start.

If the idea of a truly amicable settlement had been presented to me, the rational Billy Keenan would've signed on the dotted line immediately. But the letter Meghan sent that day was anything but amicable. The letter cast blame on me for the selfish act of surfing and putting the family's well-being in peril. She also said that my wild accusations about the Keenan Strong money were destroying the family. When Father McKeon had finished reading the letter, we both looked at each other in complete disbelief.

Most people go through their lives quite happily with little trials and tribulations along the way. Most people in the world are never confronted with malevolence. I had lived my entire life in the light. I had used the talents that God had given me to bring joy. As I look back on my life I believe that every action, every breath I took was a prayer of thanksgiving. Every pitch I threw to Kieran for batting practice was me saying thank you to God for letting me do this. Every mile I ran was a prayer of thanksgiving. *Thank you Lord for giving me the strength to do this.*

I was one of the several million people on a planet of seven billion who got to experience the sublime joy of going to the beach in the early morning and paddling out as the sun was rising. That was my happy place where I could paddle out at dawn with two or three guys while a pod of dolphins broke the surface and then dove back down 50 yards away. I would sit straddling my board and say a silent prayer. *Thank you Lord, I feel your presence.* While I was in the hospital after the respiratory crisis, a full on campaign was waged against my son Kieran. One fall Sunday, Kieran came up to my hospital room to watch football. He was in tears saying, "Daddy, you have to come home! I don't think I can take it for too much longer. Please come home!" He told me about what was being said to him. He told me that his mother had called him a "FUCKING dick head" when she had him alone in the car. He told me that he was playing with Pat at dinner and jokingly held up a knife towards Pat and his mother and grandmother began to accuse him of being psychotic and out-of-control. He reacted by screaming and crying. They were trying to get him to crack. They were attacking him to get to me. I realized because Kieran had sided with the Keenans and was clearly on his father's side, they were verbally abusing him too.

Things got so bad for Kieran one night, he was in a total meltdown and called me at the hospital. I told him to sit tight and

I called my Uncle Kevin and Aunt Barbara. They went down to the house and confronted Meghan. Uncle Kevin got in Meghan's face. "Look at me! Look at me! Is it true? Is it true? Are you verbally abusing this child?" I'm not sure if Kevin actually got a reaction out of her.

My son left the house that night with Kevin and Barbara and went to sleep in their house. He returned to our family's home the next day after school, but Meghan now realized that Kieran would speak out against her if he needed help. Kieran was living in fear, but I was his greatest ally and I would not allow him to be hurt by this woman anymore.

I remained in the hospital for a few more days before I was transferred to Helen Hayes for 10 days of respiratory rehab. While it did me good to be out of our home, my son needed me there desperately. I was in a weakened condition and needed time to get stronger, but I arrived home on December 23rd, 2015.

The Complete Blunder

One night when I was at Helen Hayes, Jim stopped by to see me. I asked if he had his iPad with him and he said he did. We rolled down into the quiet room and I proceeded to record a video for publication on Facebook. In the short, three minute video, I scorched the earth. I let the world know that the Keenan Strong money had never been accounted for and that I still did not know how much had been raised or the whereabouts of the money. I said that the one "nearest to me" had told me that the money was not for me and that it was to be used for her and the children. I also included her direct quote that she would burn it before I saw a penny of it.

Jim and I both thought the video turned out great. We were running on pure emotion and that emotion was rage. All we wanted was justice, a reckoning, and a public outing of their treachery. When I arrived home on December 23rd, Kieran was finally able to breathe a sigh of relief. My heart broke for this child. Christmas morning was an absolute disaster. With my being so weak, I directed my Mom to get Kieran a few things that were on his list. He was angry about his gifts, and lashed out screaming that he didn't get anything that was on his list, and this was the worst Christmas ever. Patrick was again shielded from all the emotions going on in the house. But he had to know that things were not right.

Meghan gave Kieran a collarless leather jacket for Christmas. He threw it aside saying, "I'm never wearing that effing thing!" For Meghan and I to be in such close quarters with the tension that existed was almost unbearable for all of us. I wanted to lash out, but held my tongue in front of my children.

Kieran's birthday, on New Year's Day, was no better. Nothing he got was any good and, to make matters worse, my wife, in her twisted thinking, put together a photo album of pictures of Kieran and her family. Once again, he reacted by throwing it aside.

Through the month of January 2016, my wife continued to abuse my Mother. Mom was routinely cursed at and shoved in the kitchen, all the while trying to carry out her duties as my caregiver. The final straw was something that seemed so insignificant at the time yet pushed me over the edge.

My Mom was sitting in the kitchen going over the schedule for my privately paid caregivers. Meghan walked into the kitchen from the family room, walked around the room, and turned off every light. My Mom stayed calmly seated, turned on her cell phone flashlight, and continued her work.

When I woke up the next day, it was a snow day. The schools were closed and my Mom told me what had happened the night before. I had seen enough. It was time to get Meghan out of the house before she caused any more harm. I called Jim and let him know that I was going to call the police. He told me to call his wife Patty to come sit with me so nothing would happen to either Mom or I while we were waiting for the police.

My sister-in-law Patty was with me in about 20 minutes. Meghan came downstairs, looked at the two of us and without a word, poured herself a cup of coffee. My wife sat down and looked at the two of us with a completely vacant stare in her eyes.

I told her, "Meghan, you will not abuse my Mom anymore. I just called the Clarkstown police about your harassment of my Mom."

She looked at Patty and me. For a few seconds, she stared through us, then said with no emotion: "I am just getting started."

The Clarkstown Police arrived and I began explaining the situation. They began to talk to Meghan and stated that what she was doing was not quite harassment, but very close. If they had to come out again, she would have to be removed from the house. Once again, her behavior was being rewarded with a lack of punishment.

I called Jim again. He got on the phone, and said one cop to another cop. "Look at my brother! Look at him! You've got to help my brother!" but he got no good answer from the police. Jim then put in a call to my lawyer. It seemed like an eternity before I got the answer I needed.

In order to get an order of protection for my Mom, the lawyers negotiated that I would have to drop the order of protection against Theresa, who had verbally abused Kieran. We decided to do so, and within an hour I was sitting in my room when I heard the door open up and Theresa announced to the house, like Jack Nicholson in "The Shining", "I am back!"

She was sitting at the kitchen table with Meghan and the two of them were laughing in complete victory. Jim was apoplectic. He made phone calls to the lawyers until the Rockland County Sheriff came with another order of protection and Meghan was shown out of the house. She left and took my son Pat with her. They were headed for Theresa's house.

You would think that this would have been the end, but in reality it was only the beginning. The pain that was inflicted on me soon engulfed my entire family.

I think that my son Kieran actually breathed a sigh of relief when his mother left. The thing that I'll never know is what effect it had on him to see his older brother walk out the door with his Mom.

I can only imagine that his 14-year-old heart felt abandoned and angry all at the same time. Patrick and Kieran had shared a room together since they were toddlers, and now they were forced onto opposing sides of a full blown battle. Through the rest of 2016 we continued relentlessly searching for the truth behind the missing Keenan Strong funds. I continued teaching at North Rockland for the remainder of the year and both the Rockland Journal News and Hudson Valley 12 TV did stories on my return to teaching. North Rockland had given me a chance to win back my dignity and I could only hope I made them proud. I gave my best every single day to honor the sacrifice all my colleagues made to give me that extra year by giving up days from their sick bank.

Once summer came around, I attended sessions at Push to Walk three days a week. Push to Walk is a privately run one-of-a-kind gymnasium dedicated to helping people with paralysis. There was a big problem. The money that had come from two small nonprofit fundraisers was all spent, and I had no more money in my account to continue my therapy. So they put me on a half scholarship. I still struggled to make the payment, marking another glaring example of how my being deprived of the Keenan Strong money had a deleterious effect on my health. I desperately needed the exercise bike and the standing frame, and yet by early August I had to stop going to Push to Walk.

If I had had the financial resources to continue attending Push to Walk, today my body would be in considerably different condition. Push to Walk gave me the opportunity to maintain both muscle tone and bone density. Simply put, both my quality and longevity of life have been severely limited by the taking of the Keenan Strong money.

In the beginning of that summer, there was an appointed day for Meghan to come into the house to get her belongings. We let our guard down and again had to pay a terrible price for it. For no rational reason, Meghan left her old Volvo S80 (she had purchased a brand new one) parked in my driveway, removed the license plates, locked the doors, and took the keys. The car could not be moved. It cost us $500 to get a new key produced so we could move the car. This stunt with the Volvo was done strictly to inflict pain and to create one more problem for us. There seemed to be no end to the havoc this woman would cause.

MVP Massacre

When Meghan vacated the house, the nursing agency was able to give me more hours to try to help make my Mom's life a little easier. They provided me with an aide from 3 PM until 7 PM and then another aide from 7 PM until 7 AM. The schedule was an absolute Godsend, and my Mom was still staying in the house to make sure that Kieran and I had everything we needed.

In early July we got a letter without warning from MVP stating that they were denying payment for my nursing services. It was the equivalent of being hit head-on by a bus without seeing it coming.

We had no idea what to do, so once again we started calling in favors from family and friends. Mom was my primary caregiver; she did everything to keep me going. She did everything for my son as well, even though at times he was openly hostile to her. He was going through a terrible time and with each question she asked, he felt that it was an intrusion. Hindsight is always 20/20, but clearly the thing for me to do was to retire even though I still wanted to work. I should have retired and started motivational speaking.

As it was, when September rolled around I got on the TRIPS bus and went back to school for a second year. The first district-wide faculty meeting at North Rockland High School was led by our Superintendent Ileana Eckert. After that, we had the high school meeting.

Dr. Gill, our Principal, began his presentation. He started to talk about the meaning of success and how the word grit comes into play. He talked about courage, fortitude, and perseverance. And then, on the screen behind him, he put up my picture from the Journal News article. Everybody clapped for a long period of time, and I felt a slight resurgence of hope.

However, going back to work for a second year was a financial disaster. We were paying $2,700 per month for privately paid caregivers to get me out of bed and ready for work in the mornings and into bed and ready for sleep in the evenings. In both the morning and the evening, it was a two person job. Mom tried to help out wherever she could, but she wasn't physically strong enough to do the grunt work. At the same time, the child support payments that I was not able to make began to rack up, as the judge had assessed my payment for two children despite the fact that one was with me, while the other was with my wife.

I truly believed that going back to work was the most noble of endeavors, but doing so. This would prove to be a financial calamity as the courts and matrimonial law seemed to mock my labor. The presiding judge looked over the financial statements at the beginning of the divorce and saw a schoolteacher making $125,000 per year and a registered nurse making $25,000 per year. There was no consideration given to the fact that the teacher was working five days a week on 4 wheels, blowing into a tube to move the wheelchair, while the nurse was perfectly able-bodied. It was becoming more and more of a battle to keep my anger from bleeding into the classroom. It was the hardest job of all to compartmentalize.

CHAPTER 15

AIDING THE FUGITIVE
BILLY KEENAN

In October 2016, on the day of the Family Court appearance, after my first class of the morning, my teaching assistant Sue pointed out that my urine catheter had backed up and was leaking urine out to the front of my pants. I called my Mom and told her we needed to get up to Good Samaritan Hospital to get the catheter changed.

I called my Family Court lawyer Kristine and told her that I was not going to be able to make the appearance. I signed into the Good Samaritan Hospital emergency room at 10:32 AM, giving the court ample time to notify the opposition that the appearance would have to be delayed. By the time I'd finished at the hospital it made no sense to return to school for the rest of the day, so we went home.

In the early afternoon, Meghan and Theresa showed up at North Rockland High School.

They barged in the main office and confronted the secretary, yelling, "We want to see the Principal! We demand to see Mike Gill!" The office secretary wanted to know who they were. Mike came out of his office, looked at the two of them, and again asked who they were. They identified themselves and told Dr. Gill to "turn over Billy Keenan immediately." They just knew that the high school was hiding me.

The following day, Dr. Gill came to my classroom for a talk, "Billy, first off I just want to know, are you okay? I knew you were going through some really bad stuff, but nobody had any idea it was this bad." I told him, "This is really scary. I never thought that they would try to get me at school. This has been my safe place. Tell me the rest of what happened yesterday." Dr. Gill said, "they accused me of hiding you at the school and insisted that I turn you over to them immediately! They then threatened me with subpoenas and lawyers." "What did you say to that?", I asked. "I told them that the school district had an entire law firm on retainer! I called the security guards to usher the two of them out of the school."

I called Jim to let him know what happened and asked him to go immediately to Rockland Family Court and take out orders of protection against Meghan and Theresa. They had violated the safety and security of my workplace and I simply could not let this kind of behavior stand. The orders of protection were served but retaliation was promptly fired back. This one hit with a damaging impact not to me, but to my brother Jim.

Theresa went to the Family Court and made the allegation that I had pulled into her driveway, rolled down the windows, and screamed the "C" word at her, which could only have happened if my mother had been driving me. If I ever said that word in my mom's presence I probably would've gotten the back of her hand—wheelchair be damned!

What Day Is It?

It was a Monday night in early October and I was getting ready for bed. I was sitting up in bed doing the nebulizer treatment and my Mom and Mary Ramos were outside in the kitchen having a chat. I looked down and I could see my right leg starting to quiver and yelled for my Mom. The quivering radiated down from my thigh to my lower leg and then from my left leg back up again. By the time it hit my knee, I was already unconscious. It was a grand mal seizure.

I woke up the next day at Good Samaritan Hospital. I was intubated and wondered why I was struggling to talk.

I opened my eyes and looked over at Jim. "What day is it?" I asked. He told me that it was Tuesday afternoon and I'd been out for about 18 hours. Once I was conscious they took out the tube and I went back to breathing normally. I was back to school on Thursday. In retrospect, it was another indication that I needed to stop, but I kept going. How many people, after suffering a grand mal seizure, would be back to work in two days?

With no money to pay the lawyers, I went to a divorce court hearing representing myself. For some unknown reason the courtroom was packed that day. Judge Alfieri was presiding over a full docket, and our case was one of the first to be heard. Jim sat in the second chair while I represented myself in what the legalese would call "pro se."

The main issue that the judge wanted to discuss that day was the delay in moving towards the divorce trial. I explained that I had to let go of my counsel due to lack of funds. He began to chastise me, but I defended myself vigorously in front of stunned onlookers, lawyers, and the people they defended and represented. I told Judge Alfieri that I was going to work five days a week on four wheels, while the opposition was going to work two days a week on two perfectly good legs. I spoke for 15 minutes. My brother Jim would later relate how he looked around the courtroom mid speech to see people leaning forward, hanging on every word.

For some reason every once in a while I find eloquence, or it finds me. I think we all have that happen to us sometimes. On that day, eloquence was met with steely resolve and Judge Alfieri gave me an extremely wide berth by allowing me to speak for 15 minutes.

At the end of my statement he looked me square in the eyes. "Mr. Keenan, the next time I see you in this courtroom you will have representation. I highly recommend that you go to Legal Aid. I'll make the call and tell them that you are on your way." When our time was over I blew into the blowpipe of my sip-and-puff wheelchair, executed a 180° turn, and began to move down the aisle. Everyone in the courtroom was looking at me and Jim, filled with stunned disbelief and admiration for what I had just done.

We took the short ride to Legal Aid and I got on the elevator, went to the second floor, rolled in, and introduced myself to the receptionist. It seemed that Judge Alfieri actually did make the call and we were expected. One of the legal aid attorneys came out and asked the first question.

"Mr. Keenan, what is your salary annually?"

"My annual salary gross is $125,000," and that was the end of the conversation. He informed me that I made far too much money to qualify for a legal aid attorney.

At this point I think it would be requisite to summarize:

- In September 2013 I was paralyzed in a surfing accident and against all medical predictions, I was able to regain independent breathing in four months.

- I survived six months in a nursing home surrounded by dementia patients.

- When I arrived home I suffered verbal abuse, physical neglect, and the revelation that the Keenan Strong money, which I now know to be over $750,000, was not to be used for my benefit.

- After a summer of withering abuse that would've broken most men, I staged a hero-like return to the teaching profession.

- I suffered several near death illnesses and made it back to the classroom.

- I watched helplessly as my family disintegrated with my sons as casualties of the war.

- I witnessed my own Mother aged 72 shoved and cursed at in the kitchen of my house.

- I lived to see security cameras attached to the wall of my family room.

- I lived to see myself too poor to afford a divorce attorney and too rich to qualify for a legal aid attorney.

- Through it all, I managed to get to North Rockland high school on the handicap accessible bus every morning with a smile.

Beware the Ides of March

On March 14th I woke up, looked out the window, and, as forecasted, there was already two feet of snow on the ground. My caregiver Ketty had stayed over the night before knowing that she wouldn't be able to get there in the snow. As she was readying the wheelchair, we detected that I was not draining urine, and what little urine was in the bag was very dark in color. I had been through enough UTIs to know that this was not good.

We waited a little while and still no urine came. My temperature was still normal, but I made the executive decision to call 911. By the time the EMTs arrived there were 40 mile-an-hour winds gusting outside in addition to the snow. They put me in a sling to bring me to the ambulance as the driveway was impassable. Due to the blizzard they were not able to get me to Good Samaritan Hospital, so instead we headed for Nyack Hospital. What should have been a 20 minute trip took the better part of an hour. When I arrived in the emergency room my temperature was up, and they began a course of intravenous antibiotics. After four hours in the ER my temperature was back to normal, and they began to print up the paperwork for discharge.

Another foot of snow had fallen and the roads were completely impassable. How I was going to get home was a complete mystery.

The discharge nurse did one more set of vital signs, and then something serious happened—my temperature had spiked in the course of an hour up to 103.7 degrees. I was admitted to the hospital, sent up to a room, and still only vaguely recall my last memory of that day entering the emergency room.

My family made it to the hospital the next day and from their accounts I was lucid, perfectly normal, and looking forward to my return home. Mom was spending most of her time making sure that Kieran was okay, while Jim spent a good deal of time in the hospital with me. But at some point on the afternoon of March 17th, things started to go south.

Jim was talking with me in the room when suddenly my eyes were wide open, rolling around in my head. I was unable to focus, simply saying, "yeah yeah yeah yeah yeah yeah yeah yeah yeah yeah yeah." I remained in this delirium for 72 hours. All of my significant family members were put on notice. They needed to be at my bedside as there was a good chance that I might not make it out of this one.

On Monday, March 20th, I came back to myself. I felt that I had been asleep for a long time when I woke up surrounded by my family. It was Monday afternoon and I looked up feebly.

"Jim..." Jim rushed over to me.

"Do you know me? Do you recognize me?" I kept telling him that of course I did. Then John got into the act and asked the same questions over and over again.

"Do you know me? Do you recognize me?"

All I could say was, "Absolutely!" I couldn't get out John's name, but everybody was excited that I made it back. Somebody ran to get the doctor and he came in and examined me. My mind was beginning to clear with each passing minute.

There was an electrode encephalogram attached to my head to monitor brain activity. I soon learned the infection that had started in my bladder had passed into my blood, and brought on the delirium. My infectious disease doctors, Dr. Chak and Dr. Anchetta, were the men who brought me back. During my time in ICU, because I was flat on my back for so long, I contracted pneumonia. This illness should've taken me, but for some reason, maybe a reason that is not for me to understand, I am still here. I endure. I suffer. I go on.

My doctors wanted to know if I was cognitively whole again so I recited the "Midnight Ride of Paul Revere" that I'd learned in third grade. After that, I wanted to know when I could go back to school again. My doctors strongly advised me to retire at that point. Just like that, the very thing that brought me back to life and gave me a purpose and a place where I no longer felt helpless but actually helpful, was taken from me. I was devastated and so tired in body and spirit. The severity of my condition was kept from Kieran, but he must've known it was fairly serious because I spent eight days in ICU and six more days in the hospital.

I returned home and went from the bed to the recliner. We were told by the wound care people to keep pressure off of my calf. The problem was, we kept pressure off my calf but both heels were resting on the recliner. I soon developed pressure wounds on both heels. This was a huge setback because I was gaining strength, but the wounds prevented me from doing anything for several months until they were cleared.

Book of Job

God loved Job and blessed him with a good wife and wonderful children. When Satan saw this, he challenged God, stating that if God took away Job's blessings, Job would lose faith in God.

So God allowed Job to lose everything. Job lost his family, his wealth, his health, and was subject to every torment that you can imagine. With each loss, Satan was sure that Job had reached his breaking point. But the story of Job is a victory. Job lost everything *except* his faith in God. God rewarded Job for passing this test of faith. In the span of two years I had become Job: I lost my health, my financial well-being, and my family.

Through all of these trials my Mom kept me faithful to God. We continued to go to the Shrine for the noon Mass, the Rosary, and the Chaplet of the Divine Mercies. I was more than a "call and answer Catholic" now. I was on my way to becoming a Christian. My mother's faith was a gift to her, it came so easily. She just believed. For me, I had to go through hell to start looking for Christ.

I saw in my life an allegory to that of Christ. The halo brace was my crown of thorns and my wife was my Judas. The pressure ulcer on my right calf was my wound, like the wound of Christ when the Roman soldiers pierced him. When Jesus endured his agony in the garden, I think he was experiencing the full view of what was about to happen. My turn in Gethsemane started with the injury and continued in bits and pieces every year that followed.

My greatest victory in my life as a Christian is that I have never given up. I see Christ in all the people who have come to my aid over the last few years—the people who helped bring me back to North Rockland, the people who bring dinner every Friday, the people who write checks every month..

Every night, almost like clockwork, I wake up at 3 AM. I take a 1mg Xanax and put on the Chaplet of the Divine Mercies on YouTube or Alexa. I go back to sleep with these words in my ears. "For the sake of His sorrowful passion have mercy on us and on the whole world." I understand His sorrowful passion. The mercy part of my story will come later.

Keenan Versus Nichols

The divorce trial started in 2017. I was the first one to take the stand, as I was the plaintiff. I had changed lawyers. I could no longer afford the first one. My new lawyer was a woman named Anna. Right away I realized that Anna was compassionate and understood my plight. She won me over minutes into the first deposition with witty remarks and quick thinking.

The first two witnesses to be called at trial were Jane Kennedy and my cousin Mary Brady. My lawyer questioned them regarding my care, but mostly about the pressure ulcer. Jane Kennedy took the stand first. Her testimony focused mainly on the lack of care shown by Meghan while she was in charge, neglecting to reposition me throughout the day to avoid such ulcers. She also shared the first encounter with my mother-in-law in the hospital when I was recovering from a UTI .

Jane testified under oath to what my mother-in-law had said to her shortly after being introduced. "It would be better for everyone if Billy died."

When I heard this in open court I simply said, "Oh my God!" Judge Thorson stopped the questioning and asked if I was okay. I simply nodded. Jane then testified that in August of 2015, while Meghan was on vacation at my mother's condo at the Jersey shore, my care was entrusted to Jane and her daughter Haley. The first morning that they were attending to me Jane saw the wound for the first time.

Jane immediately called my cousin Mary Brady who intervened and ultimately saved my life. Mary then took the stand and testified as a woman who'd been a nurse for over 20 years. She stated that a stage IV wound "could be lethal."

I took the stand at the commencement of the trial and my lawyer Anna questioned me directly. Without a moment's hesitation I went through everything that had happened down to what was said and on what date it was said. My recall was almost perfect. My attorney was well prepared and well versed with my story and asked all the right questions. I calmly recounted all of the horrors and abuses to which I'd been exposed.

Somehow I believed in the justice system. I was convinced that Judge Thorson would see my condition, understand my agony, and punish the oppressor. How wrong I was! At the conclusion of my testimony, Judge Thorson ruled against my claim of egregious conduct on the part of my wife. A victory for the opposition.

My reluctance to go to the authorities for the sake of sparing my children had once again proved to be a fatal error. Had I gone to the police, Meghan would have been removed from our home earlier. The game would have taken a completely different course. I would have had hard documented evidence of abuse, instead of just my word. My word was not enough. What Judge Thorson saw in the witness box was a man in a wheelchair. He could never have any idea what I'd lived through. No one could.

I've lived my life with very few regrets, but I do now regret listening to my Mom as opposed to my brother Jim about reporting the abuse to the police. The correct strategic move would have been to involve lawyers from the beginning, bring the Keenan Strong committee together, and demand the money. My first lawyer had played upon my raw emotions and encouraged Jim and I to make a Facebook video which backfired, then charged billable hours for his staff to view the comments made online about the video. For every comment made online, my wife's brother added the same untrue rebuttal comment, stating there was no misappropriation and that Meghan loved me and had done nothing wrong.

CHAPTER 16

THE BAGMAN

After Jane and Mary had testified, before I took the stand, Rob Smith was called as a witness. Rob was a retired NYPD Detective and the neighbor to my in-laws. Rob took the stand as what could only be described as a hostile witness to the plaintiff. Being a retired cop, he was very good in the witness box, answering the questions with minimal words and being careful not to divulge very much. He testified that at the end of the May 4th event in Orangeburg, New York, the envelopes with the money, cash, and checks were taken out of the freezer, put into a large cooler and entrusted to Rob. My in-laws slept that night in a Comfort Inn on Route 303 in Orangeburg. Rob testified that he took the cooler home to his house in Pearl River and remained awake through the night with his pistol at his side to guard the cooler. He did not open the cooler or examine its contents. Through the early morning hours there was no contact from my in-laws, but Rob finally got a hold of my father-in-law and explained that he did not feel comfortable with the cooler in his house. My father-in-law arrived shortly after taking the cooler from Rob. My lawyer then asked Rob about the fundraiser. She asked approximately how many people were at the fairgrounds. Rob answered that he did not know. My lawyer pressed the matter: would he have said that there were thousands of people there?

Rob said that there were not thousands there, maybe hundreds. He was lying, as I was there and witnessed the thousands of people gathered to support me. He was afraid of saying anything to hurt the case of his next-door neighbors.

The trial was delayed by the episode of the near fatal urinary tract infection. When the trial resumed, Anna willingly stepped back. I had a new lawyer, Don Ferrick. Don was brought in at the behest of my good friend Michael Garvey.

Don was not a matrimonial lawyer, but rather a contract lawyer. He took on my case pro bono and promised nothing more than the best outcome we could possibly get.

Don laid out a simple, streamlined case. *Forget about the money— the money is gone.* My best hope in securing a good outcome was to prove that my income was far exceeded by my monthly expenses and therefore I was entitled to the majority of the marital assets. He took all my expenses and put them on a large poster board on the easel in front of the courtroom. He never took those down in the hopes that the judge would be looking and understand that my income did not come close to paying for my monthly bills. It was a master stroke.

In the Crosshairs

The best advice my lawyer gave me was not to look directly at Joe Black, but rather to direct every answer to Judge Thorson. I continued this for my entire cross-examination.

Joe Black was a portly man with a fat face and a toupee. I often wondered in lighter moments who did he think he was fooling? He began every question with, "Mr. Keenan, are you aware...?" When I answered, I directed my response to Judge Thorson. I never gave Joe the benefit of looking at him or allowing him to goad me into confrontation. Any bitterness and anger I showed would have given him fodder to attack me even more.

While under cross-examination, opposing counsel asked "Mr. Keenan, are you aware that your Florida house was so badly storm damaged that it is un-rentable?". Something inside me knew that this question would come up in trial, so I asked my cousin Marian who lived in Delray Beach to drive to my property, and she did. Without addressing Mr. Black, I turned my attention to Judge Thorson and said "Your Honor, we have a big problem. Opposing counsel is lying. My cousin Marian knocked on the door and a woman from Pearl River opened the door and invited Marian and her father in. She told them that she had rented the house from Meghan from November until May at the price of $1,000 per month. Marian inspected the property inside and out, and found it to be in pristine condition. I thought that this would be the knockout punch, but without missing a beat Mr. Black yelled, "The only reason she had to rent the property is because Mr. Keenan would not pay the taxes." I turned my attention back to Judge Thorson, saying "Your Honor, he just said the property was unrentable, and now he is saying it was rented because I wouldn't pay the taxes!". Mr. Black then piped up again, saying "Your Honor, I am not the one testifying." Without any interruption from the judge, Mr. Black was allowed to go on with his cross-examination. This is just another example of lies and manipulations that went unpunished.

Meghan took the stand next. Joe was very careful to ask very specific questions that could be answered with one or two words. One of the most memorable questions came when he did ask about misappropriated money. Meghan leaned forward into the microphone and screeched, "I never misappropriated any money!" She was nearly out of control and screaming directly at me. What struck me most was understanding that this was a woman who never actually loved me. What she saw in me was a money-maker who gave her two children, a house, and a car. Throughout the marriage, I was often subjected to periods of silence and alienation. For years I walked on eggshells, wanting only to avoid punishment. For years I yearned to be free of this woman, and what kept me tethered to her was only my love for my two sons. I realized at this moment that I had been in an abusive marriage for years before my injury.

My refusal to go into a nursing home and to sign over the properties before the divorce had spoiled every one of her plans.

I know I've said it before, but it bears repeating. All she would have had to do was to come clean about the money, ask for a divorce, divide the properties evenly and equitably, and try to co-parent our sons as effectively as possible. I would've signed that deal in a minute. But grace, and human decency, was never offered. There must be a more humane way to divorce a quadriplegic. The opposition in the divorce called no other witnesses. To do so would serve to completely undermine their case. The great thing about the truth is that every time you repeat it, it's always the same. Meghan, Dave, Theresa, and their father Tommy would not be able to tell the same story if you asked the same questions. The opposition counsel was very wise in keeping the scope of his questions to Meghan very narrow.

My lawyer Don Feerick, asked a pointed question about the check that was written by Meghan to Joe Black in the amount of $3,800 on May 13th, 2015.

"Didn't you write this check to find out how best to divorce your husband?"

Meghan was well-prepared. "I wrote the check to help my sister pay for her divorce." This answer made absolutely no sense, as Theresa's divorce had been years ago. Her new husband used Joe Black as his attorney for his divorce. Don pressed the matter further. If Theresa needed money, why didn't Meghan just write the check to Theresa? There was no adequate answer given to this question other than Meghan mumbling something about wanting to give the money directly to Joe Black. Once again, like a dog with a bone, I couldn't let go of these questions. Theresa had more than an ample income. There was no way that she needed to borrow money from Meghan. The whole thing made no sense.

Don asked questions about Meghan's living arrangements and their cost. She stated that she felt a moral obligation to pay rent to her sister and subsequently to her mother and father. Knowing the family as I did, I believed it was unlikely that any of the Nichols charged Meghan money to live with them.

The divorce trial ended in April 2018. The lawyers sent in their summations in writing to the court by the end of May. Thus began a long period of waiting for the decision.

We were all exhausted from the trial that took three years to complete. In truth, since 2015, our lives had been consumed with getting the truth out, but even when we did, it got us nowhere. We begged the people from the committee to go public, and no one would. The bottom line: when the shit hit the fan, everybody went running for cover.

Mom Was Enraged

After my bout with urosepsis I was forced by my doctors into medical retirement. I had enough sick days to cover me until the end of June, but after that my teaching life would officially be over. What happened next was something my Mom and I never saw coming.

Meghan and her lawyer took the court order for child support up to the Department of Social Services (DSS) in Pomona and got my Social Security disability wages garnished from $2,600 down to $988. The remaining $1,612 would go to Meghan for child support in arrears. My going back to work, which was a triumph on so many levels, turned out to be a travesty financially. As for the money, there was no way around the law. There were no accommodations given because of my disability.

I thought I was doing the noble thing by going back to work to provide for my family by teaching. I was left to live on $988 per month from Social Security and a small disability pension from the New York State Teachers Retirement system. The money I received each month would be nowhere near what I needed to cover my living expenses. The word of my plight started to trickle out among the friends of my Mom from her days as a child in the Bronx. These wonderful lifelong friends began sending Mom monthly checks, helping to defray my monthly costs.

I truly believe that the one person besides me who was affected most by my abuse and the theft of the money was my Mom. All of her best efforts were for naught as the Nichols already had a carefully structured plan. With my Social Security at $988 per month and my teachers pension at $1,700 per month, I was getting $2,650 per month. We received the first two months of checks and Mom innocently opened an account with both her name and mine. A few weeks later she went to withdraw money and found that the accounts had been emptied. Anything with my name on it was subject to garnishment.

The other side got away with $5,000 clear. Mom was enraged and distraught. While my brothers Jim and John and I yearned for earthly justice, my Mom would simply say, "There is a just God waiting for them. Forgive them for they know not what they do." It was impossible to forgive the Nichols for not knowing what they did because they knew *exactly* what they were doing. They were stealing from a crippled man whom they hoped would pass sooner rather than later.

My brother Jim had warned Mom against putting the money in a bank account with my name on it, but she would say naïvely, "There is no way they would ever go after that money." Wrong again. We were able to convince Mom that when the next monthly checks came, we would have to use the check cashing business in Haverstraw on Route 9W just across from the McDonald's. I remember the day well. It provided some great levity in the midst of four years of darkness and chaos. Mom went into the check cashing place by herself, leaving me in the car. The person behind the counter refused to cash checks with my name on them, so Mom came back outside to inform me. She then brought me into the store.

I was placed in front of an Internet camera and my face was scanned so that they would have an identification. We cashed our checks, paid the fee, and went home with the money.

Making Chicken Salad

After being told I had to retire from teaching, I have to admit that I slumped into a little bit of a depression. Don't get me wrong–I was quite relieved to be home and to be alive after coming so close to my demise, but I felt that the very thing that brought me back to life was taken from me. I was at another existential crossroads. This could not be the end of Billy Keenan. Once again, for some unknown reason, I had been spared. I referred back to Steven's words that I had a role to play, that my work was not yet done.

There was a conservative talk show host named Dennis Prager. One day, while driving around in the Popemobile, I heard him talking about the writings of a man named Rabbi Steven Leder. Rabbi Leder is kind of Hollywood's Rabbi. He created a paradigm of how people are best able to transcend human suffering. He acknowledges the fact that given tragedy and trauma we all say the same thing: *Why me, God? Why? Why? Why?* Those lucky ones among us who are able to get past suffering are the ones who turn the *why* into a *what*, acknowledging that this horrible thing happened, now *what* am I going to do about it? For me the choice was obvious. I may not have been able to teach five days a week, but I'd be damned if I couldn't go out as a speaker at least once a week. I was given a huge platter of chicken shit and now it was time to make chicken salad.

In the middle of September, my colleagues and friends in the Social Studies department at North Rockland High School were kind enough to give me their classrooms to begin to build myself up as a public speaker. I started with the AP US history class.

I sat in my wheelchair in front of the class and told my story for 45 minutes. I had no slides and no script. I told my story chronologically from May 19th, 1989–the day I was commissioned a second lieutenant in the Army–to my life as a musician, teacher, triathlete, surfer, and eventually, spinal cord injury survivor. I didn't realize it at the time, but my friends were actually giving me these speaking gigs as an act of charity.

Either way, I saw the reactions of the students. After one of my first talks, a young man came up and whispered to me, "I was thinking of hurting myself before I heard your talk. Now I'm not going to." Maybe it was just the visual of me in this wheelchair seemingly happy enough to be alive, having come through so much, that gave this young man the perspective that his problems were not so bad. Whatever the case, I believed that I was onto something.

I continued giving my talks to the 12th graders before starting to incorporate slides and photographs from my former life. Eventually I streamlined my talks and I began to leave more time for questions. At the early stage of my public speaking life I did not mention the really bad stuff. It would take far too long to explain. However, the students wanted to know. Did I have a wife? What about my kids? How does your wheelchair work? The more presentations I gave, the more invitations followed. The momentum of the speaking engagements gave me a greater sense of purpose. Maybe this was the role for which my life was spared!

Speaking Up for Christ

My good friend Ed Stubbing soon invited me to give a brief talk at his 75th birthday at the Knights of Columbus in Blauvelt, New York. Ed t was filled with the light of Christ. I hadn't planned what to say when I got up to speak, so I told the 10 minute version of my story. I distinctly remember using the words "God showed up" when talking about Eric Hoblitzell (the man who pulled me lifeless out of the ocean) and Steven McDonald. I still believe that the intervention of these two men was not a happy accident; I'll never know the answer. I can never know the mind of God. However, I can identify with the suffering of Christ. I can understand that He is the source of infinite mercy and forgiveness. If I am truly a Christian, how can I not use this opportunity to help people?

The talk at Ed's party went over gangbusters and people were standing up and cheering. There was a videographer there and I was able to get the DVD. I sent the video to the President of Albertus Magnus high school in the hopes that I would be able to come and give faith witness talks to the student body.

Bob Gombrect was the President of Albertus Magnus. Bob was very gentlemanly, well spoken, and had previously been the

Principal of Fordham Prep in the Bronx. He reached out to me after receiving the DVD and invited me to do a keynote talk at the freshman retreat in March. I responded with great delight and told him that I would be there.

Dancing With the Grim Reaper

I missed the freshman retreat because I was in the hospital again. It was January of 2018 and I had a urinary problem that I'd never had before. I was at Kieran's JV basketball game on Friday evening and when I returned home found blood in my urine. After waiting an hour, blood was still filling the bag, so I called 911.

I was concerned but not stressed out yet. That quickly changed. I got into the ambulance and halfway up to Good Samaritan Hospital, I called out to the EMT.

"Dave, where are you?"

"Billy I'm right here!" I was blind. Everything looked like a whiteout and I couldn't see anything. I was rushed into the examining room and given IV fluids and the suprapubic catheter was changed. I asked my Mom to get John to come in from Long Island; my brother Jim was away. I lay there for three hours on a hospital bed and prayed.

"All right God, if this is it, into your hands I commend my spirit." My brother John arrived very quickly and sat with my mother in the examining room. They tried to remain upbeat but I could see they were as terrified as I was. As I lay there in the examining room all I could think was, "I cannot live like this. I cannot go through my life being blind and crippled. Why is this happening? My God where are you?"

After two full hours of blindness, my nurse was in the room and I looked up at her face. "Do you have dark, curly hair?" She said yes. "Are you wearing maroon scrubs?" She said yes. My vision was coming back.

After another half-hour my vision was fully restored. I don't have the words to describe the relief and joy that I felt when my sight was restored. I thought it was a miracle. In reality, when I wasn't draining urine the urine backed up and caused my blood pressure to spike, increasing pressure on the optic nerve, and thus rendering me temporarily blind. I remained in the hospital until the next day when I was discharged. I had dodged another bullet.

CHAPTER 17

PLANNING A PARTY

After a few days at home I called my friend Sister Pat Hogan, the pastoral minister at my church, St. Francis of Assisi in West Nyack. I told Sr. Pat that I'd like to get together for a meeting at the Parish Center and she agreed. When I arrived at St. Francis, I asked my Mom to let me go speak to Sr. Pat alone. Sr. Pat Hogan had been my theology teacher in ninth and tenth grade at Albertus and was a dear and trusted friend. We had visited together and prayed together many times after my injury.

"So what are we talking about today, Billy?" she asked. I smiled.

"I want to plan a party, Sister Pat!" We went into the little classrooms of the parish center and I asked her to get out a yellow legal pad. I told her that I wanted to plan my funeral. I explained the incident where I lost my sight and I felt that while I was alive right then, anything could change at a moment's notice, and I wanted to be ready.

There were certain things that I wanted for my funeral Mass and most of them had to do with the music. The first thing we did was pick out Scripture: Psalm 23. I next focused on the Gospel, for which I insisted upon the story of Lazarus. I love this gospel because in it Jesus reveals his humanity and divinity both in one moment.

Jesus was in the company of Mary and Martha as they tended to Lazarus. When Jesus left, Lazarus died. Jesus returned and Martha cried, saying, "Lord, if you had been here, my brother would not have died." Christ was so moved by the grief of Mary and Martha and, even though it was before the time of his true revelation, he acted. He called Lazarus from the tomb. Jesus was foreshadowing his own death and resurrection. For me to understand God is difficult– the vastness, the all-encompassing nature of God is beyond my intellect. Jesus, on the other hand, is someone with whom I can identify.

Sister Pat and I then planned the music, and I laid out an elaborate Irish concert to be held as a prelude to the liturgy. In thinking about it now, I think that this session should go on after the first night of the wake in the back of the rear hall. Sister Pat has all the songs and knows whom I want to sing them. I want it to be a celebration of my life and all the joy that I felt during it. I know that it will be difficult for my friends and family, and I want them to be able to hold onto each other tightly to get through what will be a difficult time.

I love my life even in this chair, and I don't want to leave. I have so much left to do. I want to live to see my sons grow into fine young men. They are my immortality, the evidence that I lived a good life, and my lasting legacy to leave this world.

On September 14th, 2013, when I stood on the deck of my surfboard riding that last wave, most of the parts of my life were good. My relationship with Meghan was similar to the Cold War policy of detente. I did what I felt I had to do to achieve peaceful coexistence. My children were happy and healthy. We had just renovated the Florida house and it was fully rented. At 46, I was stronger and faster and had more endurance than I had when I was 36. In one moment, I lost everything. If I had missed that wave, if I had been one second ahead or one second behind, the outcome of my life might have been completely different.

Mom and the Lung

Without my mother's care I would have been shelved away in a nursing home years before. When Meghan was finally removed from the house in February of 2016, Mom basically dropped everything and more or less moved into my house. My Keenan cousins often relieved her for the overnight shifts, but most nights it was Mom.

After Meghan was removed from the house we ordered a recliner so my Mom could sleep in my room. It's amazing that we hadn't thought about it before, but we were so busy fighting battles on so many fronts that it had slipped our minds. When we got the recliner and put it in my room, I asked her if I could be placed in it with her help. Mom, with the help of one of my caregivers, got me up on the Hoyer lift and sat me down on the recliner so I could watch Netflix. It was one of the happiest moments that I'd had in the seven years since my injury.

I know I'm skipping a lot here but the years of constant turmoil took their toll on my Mom. I know that she ignored her own health so that I would be able to live and get to all of my medical appointments. Every time I was hospitalized, Mom would stay late and be there first thing in the morning.

Right after Thanksgiving of 2018, I was again having difficulty clearing mucus from my lungs. I went to the doctor to get checked out and they said my lungs were clear. Later that evening, on the Friday after Thanksgiving, I was having serious respiratory distress. I went to the ER at Good Samaritan Hospital for an x-ray before being sent home. By Monday I could barely breathe and I was rushed back to the hospital in an ambulance. The CAT scan revealed a large plug of mucus in my lung that had to be cleared via bronchoscopy.

My pulmonologist arrived and snaked the tube down my nose and into my lungs. Dr. Chang continued the procedure for 45 minutes each time indicating to the nurse the dosage of sedative. He was able to clear a good bit of the mucus, but not all of it. They let me rest for a day and I decided to call my friend Ed Stubbings and ask him to get Father Tom to come to visit me at Good Samaritan. I wanted to make a good confession and talk to Father Tom about my experiences, my fears, and just my faith life in general.

Father Tom showed up, anointed me with the Sacrament of the Sick, and heard my confession. We were talking for a while before I got another great gift. After a period of alienation which lasted about a year, Kieran told his mother that he was coming to see me even though he had been forbidden by her to use his car to visit me. He arrived in my room at the hospital.

Dr. Berg from the pulmonology group came in and did the bronchoscopy for another 25 minutes on Friday. He was able to clear the mucus and showed me the plug that was lodged in my lungs. It looked like a jellyfish with tentacles. It was that thick. Little wonder that my lung had almost completely collapsed.

February 7th, 2019

On February 7th, 2019, I was waiting for Mom to pick me up for Mass at 11:30 AM. The time came and went. By 1 PM I began to wonder what had happened, so I started calling and texting but got no response. At roughly 1:30 PM, Jim called to tell me that our mother was gone.

My mother was one week shy of her 76th birthday when she died. She had been renting the apartment in the basement of my cousin Bobbie's house when Bobbie found my mother lifeless on the bathroom floor. She'd been doing a load of laundry. When Jim called me something in his voice made me think the worst. Mom would always text if she were going to be late. She had just had an appointment where they noticed her heart rate was very high, and the cardiologist had prescribed anti-seizure medication. The medical explanation was that our mother had suffered a stroke and died within seconds. It's cliché to say she didn't suffer, but I cannot help but feel that the previous four years of distress at the hands of Meghan and her family played a significant part in her death.

I felt a real sense of dread and fear of what would become of me without my Mother. I was also incredibly angry that Meghan and her family had robbed my mom of the peace she should have enjoyed in her retirement.

Everyone stepped up. My caregivers Ketty, Lauren, and Maggie all stopped by to make sure that I was okay. Not only did Mom's passing leave me without a primary caregiver, it also left me without a best friend. Mom had literally laid down her life for me.

Eighteen hours after finding out that my Mom had passed, I was awakened by my overnight caregiver at 6:45 AM on February 8th. My soon-to-be ex-wife was on the phone, screeching about how stressful the passing of my mother was on our autistic son Patrick. This woman was screaming at me as I calmly lay in bed. This was 18 hours after learning that my mother had passed— instead of being allowed to mourn my mother in peace, I was being tormented.

The next few days were like a whirlwind. We all went about executing the tasks that needed to be done to plan her funeral. The first day of the wake, I rolled up to the casket and saw my mother. That was the only time that I looked at her. I wanted to remember her as she was the last time I'd seen her.

What You Were and What You Are

The absence of my Mom left me vulnerable to even more sadness from a source that I never could have foreseen. Several of my ex-girlfriends came to offer condolences and I was instantly filled with regret that I had not married any one of them. Each girl was once everything to me, and now they each represented a dream of a lasting love unfulfilled. I was alone in my wheelchair while my brothers were with their wives. In a room filled with people I felt completely lonely. How could I have screwed up each of these former relationships? Was it just that the timing was wrong? I know a lot of my relationship problems had to do with my professional uncertainty, but I was so wrong. I was always waiting for things to be perfect to make my move; my thinking was flawed. I had so many chances to get it right. I came so close to having a lifetime of happiness.

The timing was absolutely perfect when I got my first teaching job at Albertus Magnus in 1996, and I made my move, but married the wrong woman. Now, after yearning to be free of her for so long, I was finally divorced but knew that a second chance at love was no longer a possibility.

My Speaking Life

Several of my early speaking engagements went very well, including two I did at Fordham University. On the heels of the Fordham talks, I was invited to speak to the United States Military Academy baseball team. It was during this talk on April 30th, 2019 that something truly miraculous occurred.

During every talk I make sure to emphasize the phone call with Steven McDonald. I speak about crying out to God for the mercy of a peaceful passing. During the Q&A, one of the cadets asked the following question: "Billy, can you speak more about your faith life? Has your faith increased or decreased, or do you have any left at all?"

I answered that if anything my faith had increased. I fought long and hard to keep it through each new wave of adversity. I told the cadets that I had won my faith through my suffering. At that moment, I wanted to rescue the mood of the room from one of sadness and sorrow to one of levity and unity.

"Believe me guys," I said, "I would've much rather have discovered Jesus through something like winning the lottery, but this is what I got!" The room broke out in laughter.

There were a few more questions before the team took the field for the pre-game warm-ups. "Billy, there are 10 of us who say a pre-game prayer on the field prior to each game. Would it be okay if we came back to the team room and said the prayer with you?" I was floored. These 10 young men, our best and brightest, our future warriors, came in and formed a circle around me. Everyone joined hands. The cadet who asked the question led the prayer, thanking

God for bringing me to them on that day. We said the Lord's prayer and the players took the field. This is but one in a series of rewarding events that have occurred in my speaking life. Even more, the prayers that I shared with the cadets made me feel the real presence of God in my life. It was as if He were telling me that I was on the right path.

During the portion of my talk when I addressed the abuse, the cruelty and mistreatment to which I had been subjected, I told the team that I got to a point where I felt *Unbreakable.* During the Q&A, one of the cadets asked, "Billy, when did you know or feel that you were unbreakable?". I took a deep breath and thought long and hard about the answer. I told the team that I first felt unbreakable at my mother's wake. In addition to the grief and fear of losing my constant companion and caregiver, I was experiencing terrible neuropathy, a burning and tingling pain from my knees to the balls of my feet throughout the entire wake. In a hospital setting it is always measured from zero to ten. Some days I am lucky and it is only a 2 or 3. At Mom's wake, my pain level was an 8. I told my brothers, "Guys, I am in so much pain that I'm going to position myself in the back corner of the room in case I have to make a hasty retreat before 9 PM". At the wake, many people wanted to see me and to express their condolences. I sat in the back corner with my legs elevated to try to stop the pain and with each question of "How are you?" I answered the question with the word, *Unbreakable!* This was the moment when I knew that I was unbreakable.

In July 2019, I spoke at a year-round school in Dobbs Ferry, New York. Their clientele consists, for the most part, of troubled students. Many of the students have had brushes with the law and a lot of them have special needs.

I began with two questions. "Raise your hand if you've had a really hard time in life." There were 150 students in the audience and nearly every hand in the room went up. "How many of you have wanted to give up?" Every hand in the room was up again. The next words out of my mouth were, "Me too." These kids were hurting. They needed to hear my message because the pain and suffering that so many of them experienced in their life probably led them to this place. My pain and suffering were exactly what led me to that school to be with them at that moment.

Six months after that talk, I was riding home from physical therapy and my cell phone, which is automatically set to pick up, received a call from those students. The principal, Dave Fine, said that several of the students wanted to talk to me and see how I was doing. They thanked me again for coming to their school, and needless to say, I was blown away and so grateful.

In late August 2019, I received a phone call from my friends at North Rockland High School. I was asked to deliver a talk to the senior class, the theme of which would be one's legacy. I worked for a solid week on my talk and structured my slides into a program entitled "Strategies for Building a Legacy." I thought I was really onto something.

I arrived at North Rockland the day of the program. It was going to be a 45 minute senior assembly and I asked the program coordinator how much time I had. He told me that I had 15 minutes. Holy crap! I'd prepared for 45 minutes and now I had to boil it down into a 15 minute presentation. Sitting backstage, while waiting to be introduced, my heart was racing. I really didn't know if I was going to be able to cut my talk down, but I summoned wits that I didn't even know I had. The previous six years had taught me that I could get through the roughest times, and this 15 minutes with the senior class would be a walk in the park. I rolled out onto the stage to thunderous applause.

I began my talk with a photo of my brother John and I on the evening of my commissioning. John was in his West Point uniform and I was in my class A green Army uniform. May 19th, 1989 was an incredibly proud moment in the life of my family. My Grandfather fought in the first World War shortly after arriving from Ireland, and John and I would become the first members of the family to achieve the rank of a commissioned officer in the United States Army. I expressed to these young people how much our country needed their time and talent and passion.

I shared with these wonderful young people all of the good things that happened in my life from the age of 22 to 46. I shared my life as a teacher, musician, father, triathlete, and surfer.

And then I shared the tough times–the photo of me in the hospital with a halo and ventilator, the intercession of Steven McDonald, the dramatic crawl back to the ability to breathe independently. In 15 minutes I covered my whole story and included my audience as best I could, relating my struggle to the challenges that lay ahead for them. I ended my talk by shouting the school motto, "Raider Pride!" All 600 students stood up and went wild! In that 15 minutes, I had dramatically turned a huge corner in my public speaking life. Immediately after the North Rockland talk I was approached by my friend Kevin. He saw the huge impact my message had on the students and offered to try to get in touch with some of the local schools. Kevin delivered exactly what he promised. Early in the fall I got the call to speak to the junior and senior classes at Suffern high school. This talk included an audience of over 700 students and teachers. I saw a huge opportunity and contacted my friend Terry Lynch, a professional videographer, to film the event. The presentation went extremely well and it was one of those times when you actually know that you're in the zone. I was open, able to poke fun at myself, and be serious all at the same time.

Through the entire Fall I spoke to close to 3,000 students at both public and parochial schools. Amazingly, at the public schools, during the Q&A, the subject of faith came up time and time again. Young people are looking for answers to their own questions of faith and belief. I am ever so careful in the secular setting to not preach or proselytize. However, once the question opens the door, then I go barging through.

At a talk I gave at Suffern high school in October of 2019, twenty students remained of 700 after I finished. They formed a semicircle around my wheelchair as I went from left to right taking their questions or comments. In the middle of the semicircle was a girl with dark hair, and as I turned my attention to her she simply said, "I'll pass."

After everyone had left, she remained and asked me, "Please tell me how you keep your faith." I proceeded to lay out an allegory that I had been thinking of for quite some time. I asked her if she remembered the slide with the picture of me in bed with a halo. That was my crown of thorns. I was very quick to add that I wasn't a Saint, a prophet, or the Messiah. I was the guy who would stay up all night drinking beer and singing Irish songs when given the opportunity. I was a regular guy, a sinner. I told her that I gained my faith through suffering. It was the way that I could understand Christ. I still didn't have the answers but I hadn't given up looking for them. She left, murmuring a tearful "thank you".

Just a few months after my injury I devoted all of my energy and passion into the goal of returning to teaching. I truly believed that teaching would be the fulfillment of the words that Steven McDonald spoke. "Billy, you have a significant role to play. When your rehab is over, you're going to come back and contribute." In my fight to regain independent breathing I could not see the ultimate goal for which God had spared me. Steven McDonald passed away in January 2017 and I began my speaking life in September 2017. In May 2018, I had the privilege of meeting Steven's wife Patty. We became friends and many times when we were together she would say, "that's exactly what Steven would say." I never tried to be Steven McDonald. There was only one and there will only ever be one Steven. He showed me the way forward through his example. He was truly a messenger of God, and in my very small way, I have been given the opportunity to do the same. I have been blessed by God to live a life filled with purpose after my injury. I view my speaking life as a vocation, as a calling, as something I have to do. When I was revived on that beach, God reclaimed me for Himself.

CHAPTER 18

THE ANGELS IN MY LIFE

The first great angel in my life is my older brother Jim. Jim is like "Michael" God's warrior. Jim was right by my side as we fought every day in court. Every day after the passing of our mother, any emergency fell squarely on Jim's shoulders. In short, I would not be alive without my brother Jim in my life. My younger brother John, who lives in Commack, Long Island is 90 minutes away by car. John does what he can, but because of the distance, the day to day details have always fallen on Jim. Despite the distance, John has given me the gift of some of my greatest days since my injury. He organized reunions with my high school classmates, our soccer coach Bob Walkley, and our Athletic Director Tom Collins.

My Uncle Kevin Keenan stepped in to fill the role of my long departed father. Kevin, like all of us, was outraged at the taking of the Keenan Strong money. And so he used all of his skills as a retired NYPD homicide detective to help build our case. He spent many hours chasing down bank records and gathering witness statements. Uncle Kevin felt a great sense of obligation to watch over his brother's son.

The next great angel in my life is Sue Segelbacher. Sue was my teaching assistant when I returned to North Rockland two years after my injury. After my retirement, Sue continued to be a beautiful presence in my life. We speak on the phone every few days and get together at least once a week. She continues to cut my hair and take me to movies and to restaurants. She is one of my best friends and I love her dearly.

My lawyer Don Feerick, a fellow Albertus and Fordham alum, stepped in at a critical juncture in my legal battles when I was in desperate need of strong representation. Don promised nothing more than to end the divorce proceedings with as favorable an outcome as possible. He knew there was no hope of recovering the Keenan Strong money. Don achieved everything that was legally possible, and he did it all "pro-bono".

A few weeks after my mother passed, I got a call from my cousin Bobbie who works for Verizon. She told me about a woman named Gerri Russo who had recently retired from Verizon to take care of her elderly mother. Her mother passed away, and Gerri wanted to get involved in helping me. We arranged to get together on a Saturday at my house for a meet and greet. Within just a few minutes of our meeting, we fell into wonderful conversation and, from that moment on, Gerri and I talked every few days and got together at least once a week, often more. Gerri became the driver for my speaking engagements and my workout sessions at Push to Walk. She has become one of my dearest friends.

During my Mom's wake, I was sitting in my wheelchair beside the casket and my cousin Dennis O'Keefe came through the line. He asked me if I was still watching the English Premiership Football. I answered yes and he said, "Let's get together on Saturday morning, and we'll watch the match together." Just like that, Dennis became a huge presence in my life. Besides watching English football together, he became another driver and also a photographer/videographer of my many speaking engagements. I like to think of Dennis as an older brother.

Throughout my speaking life, there have been several times when I turned to a professional videographer Terry Lynch to help document the significant speaking programs. Terry, without fail, showed up and created beautiful videos that represent the very best moments of my speaking life. He did all of this without accepting a dime in payment. What he did for me would have cost thousands of dollars. Terry is a great friend.

Since my Mother took over as my primary caregiver, our friends from the Stony Point area put together a roster of people who would bring over dinner. Without fail, every Wednesday and Friday for the last five years, a friendly senior citizen arrives at my home and provides company and a delicious home-cooked meal. After my mother passed, the group became aware of my desire to eat a very strict diet with few carbohydrates. They now text me to see what I would like to eat. They do these things for me without fanfare and without anyone knowing they are doing it. They just do it out of the goodness of their hearts, and it is greatly appreciated. With their help, I have lost nearly 50 lbs. over the course of the pandemic.

Jean Marie Healy, a high school classmate, stepped in with the offer of assistance at a critical juncture in the writing of this memoir. The publisher needed a book outline to accompany the manuscript and it was too arduous a task to attempt on my own. I needed help and Jean Marie provided that help and a great deal more. Her contribution to this memoir is invaluable. I will be forever grateful.

Once I had a finished manuscript, I needed the assistance of an editor. Lenore Gavigan, my former English teacher from Albertus Magnus, stepped in and used all of her talents to get this memoir through its final push for publication. Lenore attended a fundraiser for me in October 2022, and, while there, offered her services as an editor. It seems whenever I came to a task that I could not accomplish alone, the right person appeared.

When I finished dictating this memoir, I reached a critical impasse. I had no idea how to get the book published. I made one phone call to two longtime friends, Jeanine and Jack McGuinness. It just so happened that Jack was going through the publishing process for his book. They immediately offered any assistance that I might need. Without their help, "The Road to Resilience: The Billy Keenan Story" would never have happened. I will be forever grateful.

Finally, the last group of angels in my life are the people who upon learning of my financial plight, started writing checks to my mother on a monthly basis. They ranged from my parents' oldest friends in the Bronx to friends from the North Rockland area. They would write checks anywhere from $50-$300. One of the most generous donors was a man I served with in the Military. After my mother's passing, all the checks were written to my brother Jim. Without the help of these good people, I shudder to think what would have become of me. I am truly blessed. I think this is how God works. We all have the ability to play the role of Savior for one another. During my able-bodied days, I was a music minister in the church I grew up in and also at Albertus Magnus. I very often played the hymn "Whatsoever you do to the least of my brothers, that you do unto me".

I would be remiss if I did not acknowledge the thousands of people who turned out to the Keenan Strong fundraisers and donated with the full confidence that the money would be used for my care. Even though the money was not used for me, it does not take away for one moment what they did for me. I could not write this book without acknowledging the incredible work of the Keenan Strong committee who gave their blood, sweat, and tears to make sure that the events would be a huge success.

The road to resilience has been "a long and winding road". By definition, resilience is the ability to adapt to or overcome adversity, trauma, or major life changes. As you have read these pages, my hope is that what has come through to you is that resilience is the force that has gotten me through the worst of times. The resilience that I have was not a God-given ability, but rather a muscle that resides in each one of us. With each challenge in my life, I developed that muscle more and more. Resilience is what saw me through the trauma of my injury, the adversity that followed, and the major life changes to which I have adapted. Everyday I wake up and the first thing I do is look at the Crucifix in my room and say the following prayer "Thank you Lord for the gift of this day. Help me make something good of it in your name. Amen."

EPILOGUE

In the early days of the pandemic, I was completely isolated. People who would normally visit me were afraid to come to my home lest they transmit Covid to me. The simple fact is that if I contracted Covid, I would have died. Before the lockdown, I had a full slate of speaking engagements throughout the spring semester. All of that went away with the lockdown. Faced with this new challenge, I did what I always do. I found another way forward. For years, people I met at my speaking engagements encouraged me to write my life story. Now, I finally had the time. I purchased a USB microphone and a software program called Dragon, and I began. My goal was to dictate one thousand words per day. After three months, I planned to have 90,000 words and a book." I learned of this method from a retired Navy SEAL and best-selling author Jocko Willink. Every day I could not wait to get into my wheelchair to begin work. Let me say that again, "I could not wait to get into my wheelchair!" There were days when 2,000 words flowed out of me, and other days, when I stared at a blank screen for several hours without uttering a word. The difficult days were the days when I recalled my darkest hours of the time in the nursing home and the cruelty that I had to endure in my own home.

As I finish "the road to resilience", it is early 2023. The dark cloud of pandemic, has for the most part, lifted, and figuratively, the sun is shining once again. I am blessed to be back out on the road bringing my message to a live audience. My message is a simple one. Deep within you lives the force that will power you through the hard times. I offer the story of my life to show you the possibilities in your own life. What one person can do, another can do! My friends, there is nothing extraordinary about me. No matter what life throws at you, you can find a way forward. It all comes down to making the decision to be positive. Very often, the only thing we have control over is how we react to adversity, rejection, and defeat. In the midst of my greatest struggles, I constantly referred back to the motto of the Christophers, "it is better to light one candle than to curse the darkness".

The battle that I have faced has been a daunting one. The injury, alone, could have taken away my will to live. The six months of my captivity in the nursing home could have taken away the will to live. The abuse, the betrayal, and the loss of the Keenan Strong money could have taken away my will to live. I made a conscious decision to keep moving towards the light. The best example that I can come up with is from the film "The Shawshank Redemption" wherein the main character Andy Dufresne uses a tiny rock hammer to dig a tunnel from his cell to a sewage pipe leading to freedom. Andy Dufresne crawled through 500 yards of raw sewage to emerge into freedom. He emerged from the sewage pipe into a storm that washed away the refuse. This is how I feel about the nine year journey that I have traveled. Now that I've emerged into the light, where do I go from here?

What I wanted most, but sadly never found in my married life, was actually being loved. Those desires have been replaced with the burning desire to show love for my fellow human beings. I have set aside the idea of romantic love and I'm working towards being able to constantly express agape, unconditional love for my fellow man. This is the highest form of love and comes from the way that God loves man. My "love songs" will be the words that I speak at my upcoming speaking engagements, and the words that I write in the future. It will not always be an easy endeavor and, as I am still a man, there will be times of longing and loneliness. When these times come in your life, my greatest hope is that you will refer to this memoir to find the inspiration that will lift you up. This is my legacy, a gift that will live long after I'm gone.

KEENAN STRONG:
AFTER-THE-FACT

The most difficult aspect of the divorce was that it rapidly devolved into a "he said-she said" regarding the Keenan strong fundraiser. The purpose of the following section is to present affidavits from key players of the committee supporting the validity of my allegations. In an article in the *Irish Voice* newspaper, Theresa, in her role as family spokesperson, denies my claims, and in rebuttal, goes on record with amounts she says were brought in by Keenan strong. Finally, I will present a summary of the findings of Stephen Kaplan, the court-appointed forensic accountant charged with getting to the bottom of Keenan strong.

The affidavits sworn to and admitted to the court records:

Patrick K., Committee member who worked diligently on the Mineola event, May 3 stated:

- Raffle ticket sales at the Mineola event were $23,500
- Amount of money taken in at the event not including the Raffles, $26,570
- Total $50,070
- The fact that the committee was never brought back together again for a transparent reporting of the funds "leaves a huge QUESTION MARK!"

Catherine D., Committee member and longtime friend of the Nichols' family, especially of Megan and Theresa stated:

- That Theresa, during the planning phase of the benefits, often used the phrasing "my sister's money", "money for my sister", or "This is for my sister"
- The committee was never brought back together after the event.

Pat D., Integral part of the committee who organized the entertainment schedule, production of my CD, and established a social media platform and presence stated:

- That "Theresa was intricately involved in the planning and operation of the events and in the handling of the donations
- During the week following the event, exchanged text messages with Theresa, such as
- "How did we do?"
- Theresa answers, "$600,000 and they're still counting". Next message, "You're not going to believe it! They are at $650,000 and still counting! You know what a pro dad is at counting cash!"
- Final message regarding tally of funds. "Hey, I don't want this getting out. They are at $750,000 and still counting. There is more money still coming in, so it looks like it will be more. Do not tell Martin!"
- Pat is delighted at $750,000 and counting, but perplexed as to why Martin should not be informed, as he was a key member of the committee and worked diligently to ensure its success.

Ken V., Irish musician, key member of the committee, organized set up of sound systems, scheduling the music schedule stated:

- Prior to the event, Theresa says, "I don't want Billy's brothers anywhere near the money. I don't trust them!"

- Perplexed by this request, decided to mind his own business and continued working to make the event successful

- During the week after the event, inquired about the final tally., Theresa says, "$700,000 and still counting"

- Communicates the importance of a "thank you" party and disclosure of the final tally for the committee.

- Theresa said she doesn't know when this meeting would take place

The *Irish Voice*
In August, 2016, I conducted an extensive interview with this newspaper to raise awareness as to my suspicion of financial fraud. Theresa was given ample opportunity for rebuttal.

- Teresa claims that I was given access to the money and kept in the loop as far as how much was raised

- States that the total number for the three events was $ 245,347.000. as enumerated below

- States total for the Mineola event $22,670

- Total for Rory Dolan's Yonkers event total $30,000

- Total for German Masonic event $181,323

- States that Martin was the true chairman of the committee and as such had the responsibility for bringing the committee together for a roundup, which never happened.

The Kaplan report

As part of the divorce, both parties were compelled to pay for a forensic accountant to conduct an investigation into the matter of the Keenan Strong fundraisers. The forensic accountant was Stephen Kaplan. Below are some of his findings.

- The focal point of the controversy was how much money was actually raised at the Keenan strong events, in particular the event held at the German Masonic Fairground in Tappan, New York May 4, 2014

- Another source of controversy was the question of whether the benefits were held for Billy Keenan's medical care or for Billy Keenan and family.

- Affidavits from Patrick and Ken were determined to be hearsay and not given consideration

- The majority of money collected was cash currency and it was difficult to determine the amount

- In the aftermath of the events, there was no notification to those involved as to the level of success achieved

- "Problematically and surprisingly, given the high-level organization that had preceded the events, there is a lack of appropriate accountability of the funds collected"

- Theresa, in charge of the counting room, says that a counting machine was used

- Eyewitness accounts refute this, saying that no counting machine was used

- No armored car/impartial third party handled transport of money

- Money received from the sale of $100 raffle tickets is completely unknown, no accounting of the number of tickets released nor the names of the volunteers who sold tickets the majority of proceeds were in cash

- Teresa states that the total received from the of raffle tickets was just over $31,000, yet one man, Kevin O'Neill, sold $20,000 by himself, outside of the fund-raising events, and numerous other volunteers from the community also sold tickets

- Kaplan refers to the accounting procedures of the raffle tickets as "wild West", suggesting that there was no control at all

- Kaplan concludes report by giving the estimate of $621,966-$645,518, exclusive of unidentified cash

After reading through the affidavits, the newspaper article, and the Kaplan report, I am left with many questions. The affidavits are very revealing in that Pat D., Ken V., and Catherine D., have long histories of friendship with both parties. In fact, all three have longer histories of friendship with the Nichols' family than they do with me. There was a high level of secrecy regarding the amounts raised at each event. The fact that Teresa does not want Martin to know the tally is very revealing because he is a close friend of me and the Keenan family. Martin had been hand-picked by me to head the Keenan Strong Committee and if he knew the amount raised, he would have definitely communicated that finding to the Keenan family. As far as Patrick K's. affidavit, the most significant piece of information is the dollar amount of raffle tickets sold at the Mineola event. He reports that $23,500 of raffle tickets were sold.

Findings of the Kaplan report. Throughout the report, Mr. Kaplan makes reference to the lack of proper accounting procedures, particularly in light of the meticulous planning of the event. Also, in the Kaplan report there is a $31,000 amount reported by Theresa assigned as the total sale of raffle tickets. This just doesn't make sense. $23,500 raised at the Mineola event and $20,000 sold by Kevin O'Neill privately total $43,500. This is $12,500 above the amount reported by Teresa. There were numerous volunteers selling raffle tickets throughout the tri-state area, which strongly suggests that the amount reported is drastically understated.

My brother Jim was in possession of all of the affidavits and the Kaplan report. He was very reluctant to share this information with me, knowing what it might do to me. He was right to be reluctant. As I read through all of these documents, I came away convinced that there was a plan in place all along to keep the money for Megan and the children. My needs were not considered. By instructing Pat D. not to tell Martin strongly suggests an effort by Theresa to keep the amount raised a secret, especially from me and my family. When I asked how much was raised one week after the event, I suffered verbal abuse and was taken back to the nursing facility without knowing the amount.

The greatest source for the misinformation is Theresa, herself. When reporting the amount raised, she uses three different numbers. To the newspaper, she uses $245,347.00. To Ken V., the number is $700,000 and counting. To Pat D., the number is $750,000 and still counting. Additionally, in the text message exchange with Pat D., she mentions that "they" are still counting and that "dad is a pro at counting cash". I was not present at the final count, nor was anyone in my family nor anyone representing my interests.

The Kaplan report also shed light on the controversy over who headed the Keenan Strong committee. The report left no doubt in my mind that it was Theresa who was in charge of the committee. Significantly, Mr. Kaplan refers to a ledger submitted by Theresa which indicated that there were two pages. However, page 2, the page that held all of the denominations and amounts, is missing. He is careful not to assign blame for the missing page, but I am left wondering why it was omitted. After an exhaustive investigation, during which Mr. Kaplan expressed surprise and concern at the overall accounting practices used, he still comes up with a number of approximately $621,000-$645,000.

After hundreds of thousands dollars were donated, I remained isolated in the nursing facility for 3 ½ more months. The only reason I was brought home was that the insurance stopped paying. When I returned home, there was no money made available to me to hire a caregiver to reposition me during the night. There was no money made available to me to purchase the equipment for a home gym. There was no money made available to me to purchase an iPhone with Siri so I could communicate with friends and family.

There was no money made available to me to purchase a desktop computer with Dragon software so I could communicate with the outside world via email or Facebook.

During the divorce, together with my brother Jim and my uncle Kevin Keenan, I took my case to the Rockland County district attorney. My thinking was that if the detectives took the individual members of the Nichols family, Tommy, Teresa, Dave, and Megan in separate rooms and questioned them, there would be glaring inconsistencies in their story. The assistant district attorney promised that his office would conduct a thorough investigation. Unfortunately, they conducted a perfunctory investigation and did not bring one witness in for questioning. One of the detectives approached Meghan in the parking lot of the medical office where she worked. She immediately told the detective to talk to her lawyer. The detective declined to bring her in for questioning, even with her attorney. After nearly 6 months, the ADA brought us in to tell us that they were not able to come up with sufficient evidence to pursue the case. Another crushing blow!

As I bring this memoir to close, I am left with very conflicted feelings. I wondered to myself, "Why? Why would they do such a thing?" What it comes down to, I believe, is that they thought so little of me, they thought that I would never stand up and fight. I wonder how differently my life would have turned out if I'd been given even half of the money. There would have been plenty of money to build a home gym that would have kept me physically fit during the pandemic. As it turned out, the pandemic was brutal on the unfortunate population to which I belong. I now suffer from numerous medical conditions that no amount of therapy will make better. These conditions preclude additional physical therapy, which means I must prepare myself for the decline that has already begun.

As with all things in my life, when adversity presents itself, I draw on the reserve of resilience that has built up over the course of my life. I will focus on what I can do rather than what I can no longer do. The best that I can come up with is that I live to serve my Savior by serving his children. He calls me to forgive and in this calling to date, I have failed. From the cross, Jesus said, "Father, forgive them for they know not what they do." In my case, I have not been able to forgive because they knew exactly what they were doing. Upon seeing the thousands gathered that day, did they ever say to themselves, "Who are these people here for." The only thing that I have control over is how I have reacted to all of this. The way I reacted speaks for itself.

ABOUT THE AUTHOR

Billy Keenan had a perfect life. He was a successful teacher, veteran, triathlete, band leader, husband, and father. A tragic accident robbed him of that ideal life. Sadly, the accident was just the beginning. In the next few years, Billy faced betrayal, abandonment, theft, and hardships that would break an ordinary man.

But Billy Keenan is no ordinary man. He is fond of quoting the Christophers' motto, "It is better to light one candle than to curse the darkness." Billy embodies the essence of that idea and has dedicated his life to inspiring others with his strength, faith, and indomitable spirit.

In The Road to Resilience: The Billy Keenan Story, he shares his incredible experiences with the world. Billy's story is not a story of a victim but of a remarkable individual who has faced tremendous adversity and found a way forward. You cannot get to know Billy without being touched and transformed.

Made in the USA
Middletown, DE
27 July 2023

35824609R00120